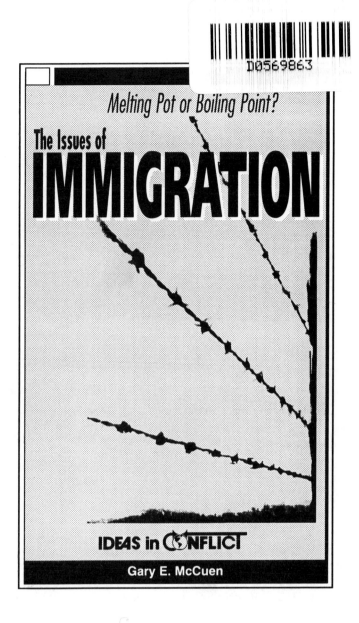

Melting Pot or Boiling Point?

The Issues of

IMMIGRATION

IDEAS in CONFLICT

Gary E. McCuen

GARY McCUEN
publications inc.

411 Mallalieu Drive
Hudson, Wisconsin 54016
Phone (715) 386-7113

Illustration and Photo Credits

Carol ★ Simpson 101, 117, 130; Department of Health and Human Services 123; Government Accounting Office 111; Immigration and Naturalization Service 19, 95; Steve Kelly 41, 81; Jeff MacNelly 55; Steve Sack 87; Social Security Administration 49, 75; Richard Wright 33.

MAY   8 1997

© 1997 by Gary E. McCuen Publications, Inc.
411 Mallalieu Drive, Hudson, Wisconsin 54016

(715) 386-7113

International Standard Book Number
0-86596-141-7
Printed in the United States of America

CONTENTS

Ideas in Conflict

REASONING SKILL DEVELOPMENT

These activities may be used as individualized study guides for students in libraries and resource centers or as discussion catalysts in small group and classroom discussions.

IDEAS in CONFLICT

This series features ideas in conflict on political, social, and moral issues. It presents counterpoints, debates, opinions, commentary, and analysis for use in libraries and classrooms. Each title in the series uses one or more of the following basic elements:

Introductions that present an issue overview giving historic background and/or a description of the controversy.

Counterpoints and debates carefully chosen from publications, books, and position papers on the political right and left to help librarians and teachers respond to requests that treatment of public issues be fair and balanced.

Symposiums and forums that go beyond debates that can polarize and oversimplify. These present commentary from across the political spectrum that reflect how complex issues attract many shades of opinion.

A *global* emphasis with foreign perspectives and surveys on various moral questions and political issues that will help readers to place subject matter in a less culture-bound and ethnocentric frame of reference. In an ever-shrinking and interdependent world, understanding and cooperation are essential. Many issues are global in nature and can be effectively dealt with only by common efforts and international understanding.

Reasoning skill study guides and discussion activities provide ready-made tools for helping with critical reading and evaluation of content. The guides and activities deal with one or more of the following:

RECOGNIZING AUTHOR'S POINT OF VIEW

INTERPRETING EDITORIAL CARTOONS

VALUES IN CONFLICT

WHAT IS EDITORIAL BIAS?

WHAT IS SEX BIAS?

WHAT IS POLITICAL BIAS?

WHAT IS ETHNOCENTRIC BIAS?

WHAT IS RACE BIAS?

WHAT IS RELIGIOUS BIAS?

*From across **the political spectrum** varied sources are presented for research projects and classroom discussions. Diverse opinions in the series come from magazines, newspapers, syndicated columnists, books, political speeches, foreign nations, and position papers by corporations and nonprofit institutions.*

About the Editor

Gary E. McCuen is an editor and publisher of anthologies for libraries and discussion materials for schools and colleges. His publications have specialized in social, moral and political conflict. They include books, pamphlets, cassettes, tabloids, filmstrips and simulation games, most of them created from his many years of experience in teaching and educational publishing.

CHAPTER 1

THE GREAT IMMIGRATION DEBATE: AN OVERVIEW

READING

1

INTERNATIONAL IMMIGRATION:
LAWS IN FRANCE, GERMANY, CANADA AND AUSTRALIA

John Guendelsberger

John Guendelsberger is a professor of law at Ohio Northern University College of Law in Ada, Ohio.

■ **POINTS TO CONSIDER**

1. How are French immigration laws and policies different from those of America?

2. Describe the Australian point system.

3. What method do Canadians use for selecting immigrants?

4. Describe Germany's attitude toward immigration. What is a guest-worker?

John Guendelsberger in testimony before the House Judiciary Committee, May 17, 1995.

All four countries reviewed also admit significant numbers of immigrants for employment and for humanitarian reasons (asylee and refugee).

I. THE FRENCH SELECTION PROCESS

The framework law for French immigration was enacted in 1945. Although many times amended, it remains an astonishingly compact document (36 articles) when compared to the American statute (Title 8, U.S.C.). As in this country, the three pillars of French immigration are family, worker, and refugee/asylee categories.

French immigration law contains no quotas, no annual ceilings, no preference categories and no waiting lists. Nor does French law draw such a sharp distinction between immigrants (permanent entrants) and nonimmigrants (temporary entrants) as does the United States law. An alien who intends to remain in France for longer than three months must obtain a *carte de sejour* (residence card) from the local prefecture. A residence card will be granted only upon proof of appropriate student, worker or family status. The residence card, ordinarily issued for just one year, is renewable through the local prefecture so long as the purpose of the visit remains to be accomplished.

French immigration has shifted during the last three decades from the worker category to the family and refugee categories. Nearly 70% of immigrants in the 1960s and 1970s entered as "workers." That figure declined to an average of 35% of entrants by 1980 and then to about 20%, where it stands today.

In comparing French and American immigration, it is important to keep in mind differences of scale. The land mass of France is about 1/17th that of the United States. French population is about one-fifth, but its population density is about four times that of the United States. Thus, if land mass were the benchmark for comparison, the United States would have to double its current immigrant quotas in order to match the French intake. If population were the benchmark, the United States would have to take in 600,000 immigrants to keep pace with the French.

II. GERMAN IMMIGRATION

Germany does not consider itself a country of immigration. In the past it has resorted to use of "guestworkers" to fill labor needs that could not be met by German citizens. Guestworkers were admitted as temporary residents whose work permits could be renewed so long as their labor was needed. In fact, large numbers of guestworkers remained for years and raised families in Germany. Because Germany recognizes no *jus soli* (law of the soil) citizenship and has very stringent naturalization laws, many second and third generation "guestworker" children (primarily of Turkish origin) live in Germany today as resident aliens.

Germany recently amended its naturalization laws to allow resident aliens between the ages of 16 and 23 who have lived at least eight years in Germany to become citizens if they have no criminal record and have given up or attempted to give up their prior nationality. A transition rule also gave resident aliens of fifteen years a presumptive claim to naturalization which could be asserted through the end of 1995.

The German Constitution explicitly provides that "marriage and the family shall enjoy the special protection of the state." (*Grundgesetz*, Article 6(1)). In a number of cases, the German Constitutional Court has held that Article 6 protections apply to resident aliens in the context of immigration. The German Aliens Act (*Auslandergesetz*) provides for family unification for German citizens and for long-term resident aliens. German citizens may be joined by a spouse and minor children. The foreign parent of a minor unmarried German child may enter and remain in Germany to exercise custody rights so long as the German parent resides in Germany. Beyond these immediate family members, a German citizen may seek entry or stay of extended family members by demonstrating "extreme hardship" (*besondere Harte*).

Family unification for resident aliens is somewhat more restrictive than for German citizens. Essentially the same categories of close relatives may enter and remain. However, as in France, the family member settled in Germany must have adequate lodging (so many square meters per person, required ceiling height, etc.) and must have sufficient resources to support the incoming relatives. More extended family members may join resident aliens in Germany if they can demonstrate that separation would cause extreme hardship.

III. THE CANADIAN SELECTION PROCESS

In the Canadian Immigration Act, the Canadian Parliament has largely delegated responsibility for selection of immigrants to the Immigration Minister. The Act sets out general immigration objectives including demographic goals, family unification, refugee protection, the fostering of trade and commerce, tourism, cultural and scientific activities and international understanding, among others.

The Act provides for three major categories of immigrants: (1) family-sponsored, (2) refugee, and (3) independent. The independent class includes skilled workers and business applicants. The selection process and the number limits for each of these categories is determined yearly by the administration. In general, the executive is directed to select immigrants in the independent category by assessing the degree to which applicants will be able to become "successfully established" in Canada.

A unique feature of the Canadian Act is its requirement that the Immigration Ministry consult with each province in formulating the annual quotas for each category. Each province may enter into a plan with the Ministry to accept varying levels of immigrants in particular categories. Under their respective plans, the provinces participate in the selection of refugees, investors, or independent immigrants who have designated that province for settlement. For the independent category of immigrants, provinces may, within limits, design and apply their own selection standards.

Canada has recently admitted about 250,000 immigrants per year. The United States, with about ten times the Canadian population took in about one million immigrants in 1992. Canada has been one of the world's leading immigrant nations throughout the last decade, admitting per capita well over twice as many immigrants as the United States.

IV. THE AUSTRALIAN POINT SYSTEM

Australia utilizes a point system selection process much like Canada's. Close family members of permanent residents are permitted to immigrate without regard to points. These relatives include:

(1) spouses and fiancées,

(2) parents,
(3) unmarried children.

Non-dependent children and siblings may immigrate if they are sponsored and score the required number of points under the point selection process.

As in Canada, family members must be sponsored by an Australian relative who provides assurance of support and assistance in settlement. Sponsorship is normally for a period of ten years. No qualifying period of residence is required of citizen sponsors or resident aliens seeking entry of a spouse or minor dependent child. Resident aliens must have lived in Australia for at least two years before sponsoring entry of parents or siblings.

Immigrants entering Australia under the labor and business migration categories are evaluated under the point system. The Department of Employment establishes quotas for various occupational categories and employers may work with the government to obtain entry of specific workers with skills not available in the local labor market. Like Canada, Australia has encouraged entry of entrepreneurs and investors. It also provides for refugees and asylees and for special humanitarian programs.

The Australian point system evaluates worker and independent applicants under the following seven categories with maximum points per category as indicated:

1. Skills 10
2. Employment 10
3. Age 8
4. Education 8
5. Employment record 10
6. Economic prospects 28
7. Growth area 6
Total possible points 80

To qualify for immigration under the selection system, applicants must score 60 points or more. Under the economic prospects category, applicants who are fully sponsored by an Australian citizen score 28 points; those sponsored by a resident alien score 25 points. As in the Canadian point selection process, the Australian regulations contain complex and detailed instructions for allocating points under each of the seven categories.

V. CONCLUSIONS

The four countries reviewed permit immigration for a category of close family members (at least the spouse, minor children and parents) of both citizens and permanent resident aliens. None of these countries places quotas or ceilings on the entry of these relatives when entering to join either citizens or resident aliens. The American selection process affords immediate entry for these close relatives of citizens, the "immediate relative" category, but requires long waits for visas under the second preference category for the spouse and minor children of permanent resident aliens.

In France and Germany, the entry of close family members of resident aliens is subject to proof that adequate housing and resources are available. In Canada and Australia, the petitioning family member promises to provide support during the initial years after entry.

These countries also provide for family immigration beyond the spouse and minor children. In Canada and Australia, extended family immigration (siblings, aunts, uncles, nieces, nephews) is permitted under the point system selection processes. In Germany, extended family relatives may immigrate in cases of extreme hardship. Both Germany and France provide for entry of family members of European Union nationals under the terms of the free movement provisions of EU law.

In addition to family immigration, all four countries reviewed also admit significant numbers of immigrants for employment and for humanitarian reasons (asylee and refugee). Notably, in each of these nations the Immigration Act delegates to the executive branch the determination of the appropriate balance in terms of numbers of immigrants accepted each year and the proportion of immigrants in the family, worker and refugee categories. Only in the American statute are such details provided at the legislative level.

AMERICAN IMMIGRATION: HISTORY AND OVERVIEW

Demetrios G. Papademetriou and Stephen H. Legomsky

Dr. Demetrios G. Papademetriou is a senior associate and director of the International Migration Policy Program at the Carnegie Endowment for International Peace, Washington, DC. He chairs the Migration Committee of the Paris-based Organization for Economic Cooperation and Development, has been an adviser to numerous U.S. and foreign organizations, and has published widely on immigration.

Dr. Stephen H. Legomsky is a professor of law at Washington University in St. Louis, MO. He is the author of a law school textbook Immigration Law and Policy *and other books on immigration and justice. He has been an immigration adviser to various American officials and organizations, and to the Russian government.*

■ POINTS TO CONSIDER

1. How has Congress sought to influence the ethnic composition of immigration?

2. Describe three ways the U.S. has used to curb illegal immigration.

3. What was the national origins quota system?

4. Define employer sanctions. Summarize the problems associated with them.

5. Explain the meaning of Proposition 187.

Demetrios G. Papademetriou and Stephen H. Legomsky, "Immigration and Civil Rights," **Civil Rights Journal**, Fall, 1995.

Editor's Note:

- *See this book's appendix for summaries of 1996 laws that have reformed immigration in major ways, and drastically limited public assistance for immigrants by many billions of dollars.*

- *Two major pieces of legislation dealing with immigration were passed in the 104th Congress. **The Welfare Reform Act,** H.R. 3734, contains provisions that curtail benefits for legal aliens and denies most benefits for illegal aliens. This bill was signed into law by President Clinton on August 22, 1996.*

- *On September 28, 1996, Congress passed H.R. 3610, **The Omnibus Appropriations Act,** which incorporated the provisions of H.R. 2202, **Immigration in the National Interest Act.** The primary objective of this bill is aimed at controlling illegal aliens. President Clinton signed this bill on September 30, 1996.*

- *The articles in the following three chapters reflect the heated national debate that led to major immigration reform laws signed by the President in August and September of 1996.*

Trite as it might be to say, the history of America is the history of immigration. Immigration, however, has not been a smooth, steady stream. Rather, immigrants have come to the United States in waves that have typically coincided with turmoil in the countries they have left behind.

The reaction of the American public has been correspondingly dualistic. We embrace the idea of immigration even as we bemoan whatever group of immigrants is most visible at the time – and we compare the most recent arrivals unfavorably to their predecessors. To better understand the history and current context of immigration-related denials of civil rights within our shores, it is helpful to deal with legal and illegal immigration issues separately.

LEGAL IMMIGRATION

With enough asterisks, it is possible to describe the first century of United States history as one of open borders. Congress did not enact permanent immigration restrictions until 1875. Since then, the restrictions have grown broader and more complex. Of the many trends that could be noted, two are particularly germane here.

First, Congress has always sought to influence the ethnic composition of the immigrant stream. In the late 19th century, Congress passed a series of statutes that selectively disadvantaged Chinese laborers. Later legislation extended many of these restrictions to the Japanese and other Asians.

The most pervasive of Congress' techniques for influencing the ethnicity of the immigrant population was the national origins quota system, in place from 1921 to 1965. Under that system, the number of Americans who could trace their ancestry to a particular country determined the numerical ceiling on annual immigration from that country. The practical effect was to dampen immigration from southern and eastern Europe.

In 1965, one year after passage of the Civil Rights Act, Congress replaced the national origins quota system with a uniform limit of 20,000 immigrants per year from any one country. A uniform per-country limit, determined by statutory formula, remains in effect today. Beginning in 1986, Congress began enacting temporary, *ad hoc* legislation to admit additional immigrants from previously low-immigration countries.

There has been a second, simultaneous trend. While Congress has been enacting selective immigration laws, aliens have been busy testing the constitutional limits of Congress' powers. The Supreme Court has responded with what has come to be called the "plenary power doctrine." When Congress legislates in the field of immigration, the Court has repeatedly said, special judicial restraint is necessary. In sharp contrast to its usual practice, the Court has consistently upheld federal immigration statutes that explicitly discriminated on the basis of race or gender, or that restricted political speech even in the absence of "clear and present danger," or that denied a hearing or even an explanation to a 25-year lawful permanent resident alien who had been excluded and detained upon returning from a temporary visit abroad.

In the past few years, the civil rights of immigrants have both expanded and contracted. On the positive side, Congress in 1986 passed a major legalization program and in 1990 passed legislation that significantly enhanced the rights of immigrants to be reunited with their spouses and their children. The same act also narrowed the criteria for excluding aliens on the basis of their political beliefs, statements, or associations, although substantial restrictions remain.

ILLEGAL IMMIGRATION

Nowadays, when the United States public debates immigration, comments tend to focus intensely on those immigrants who are here illegally. In a nation built on the rule of law, that emphasis is not surprising. Yet the overwhelming majority of immigrants enter through regular legal channels and remain in lawful status.

From a world perspective, most human migration has taken place outside systematic state regulation. This has happened in part because most major migration movements occurred before the formation of the nation-state. But even after states came into being, migration to the New World remained largely unregulated until early in the 20th century. Even today, despite stringent regulation of entry, much migration continues to take place outside state controls.

In the United States, eight years after Congress made legal the presence of nearly three million aliens, an estimated four million aliens are unlawfully here. Unauthorized migration is thus the number one U.S. immigration challenge. Because policy responses to that challenge have increasingly significant civil rights implications, the responses require the rigorous and exacting attention of the civil rights and civil liberties communities.

U.S. responses to illegal immigration have focused on three areas: border controls, employer sanctions, and restriction of benefits.

Border Controls. Improved U.S.-Mexico border security is now again a premier strategy of control. Rhetorically at least, the strategy had been a long-standing priority for successive U.S. administrations. Since adequate resources were never appropriated, however, the likely effectiveness of this strategy is still unknown.

Employer Sanctions. Only about half of America's unauthorized immigrants enter the United States illegally; the other half enter lawfully as temporary visitors but then overstay. Tighter border controls might reduce the size of the first group, but they will not appreciably diminish the second. Employer sanctions, in contrast, are directed broadly. Their premise is that, push factors aside, jobs are what attract unauthorized aliens to industrial soci-

18

Naturalization Applications Filed Nationwide

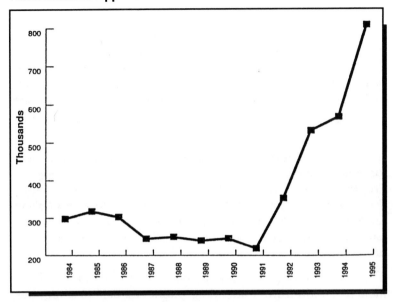

Source: Immigration and Naturalization Service

eties. Access to jobs had been relatively unhampered until recently. Nearly a decade after the enactment of employer sanctions, two questions remain unanswered. First, have sanctions reduced unauthorized employment? Second, have they spawned job discrimination based on ethnicity?

The answer to the first question is that while employer sanctions may have complicated the employment searches of unauthorized workers, they have not curbed appreciably the flow of new unauthorized aliens into the U.S. labor market. That is because the social mechanisms that connect employers with foreign workers are primarily family and friends. Sanctions have simply made these networks more important than before. Moreover, sanctions induce many foreign workers to obtain fraudulent documents.

The discrimination question has two components: hiring decisions and wage differentials. The latter is simpler to discuss. Reducing the wages offered to foreign-looking or -sounding workers is a tempting way for employers to pass on their increased costs of monitoring the workplace – actual or expected. In addition to the "fairness" and social policy concerns that all discrimi-

19

nation raises, labor market discrimination lowers labor standards for all workers and requires action to redress it.

Hiring discrimination is more complex. Employer sanctions might simply reinforce the existing ethnic or national-origin biases of some employers. More alarming, however, sanctions might deter some employers from hiring "foreign-looking and -sounding" workers out of fear of liability. Both government and private sector reports have found significant evidence of precisely such discrimination.

Restriction of Benefits. The most dramatic single development for undocumented aliens in the past year has been the passage of Proposition 187 by the voters of California. That initiative declares undocumented aliens ineligible for a range of publicly funded services. It also requires state health, education, and welfare officials to perform specified investigation and enforcement functions.

The best known provision of Proposition 187 prohibits undocumented children from attending public schools and requires school district officials to investigate the immigration status of all enrolled children and their parents. Students or parents who are suspected to be without legal status must then be reported to the Immigration and Naturalization Service (INS). Since the Supreme Court struck down a somewhat similar Texas statute in 1982, the implementation of Proposition 187 has been stayed pending a final decision on its constitutionality.

CONCLUSION

In the end, none of the immigration policies discussed in this article will solve the unauthorized immigration "problem." Issues will remain as long as there exist egregious economic disparities among countries – particularly between contiguous countries that share extensive historical migration relationships.

Therein lie the roots of unauthorized population movements. Absent their improvement, even Draconian control measures will fail to reduce illegal immigration substantially. And in attempting reductions, such measures may damage other values our society holds dear.

Responding responsibly to the challenge of trans-national migration is an immense test that requires the thoughtful and sustained care of all members of the world community. To meet the challenge, we must understand properly both the structural causes of migration and the personal ambitions and aspirations of those who move. Whether the issue is one of the most appropriate border or labor market controls, expanding or creating channels of regular immigration access, safeguarding the human, social, and labor market rights of all workers, affirming protections for *bona fide* refugees, or working cooperatively to achieve measurable progress in the development of the "South," the only viable long-term solution is international cooperation that protects human dignity while safeguarding each country's actual or potential interests.

In addition, policymakers everywhere must remember that the purpose of law is to protect all people who are in fact within a state's political jurisdiction. To do anything less would in the long run undermine the character of the polity in ways that would be far more consequential than the temporary discomfort imposed by unauthorized immigration.

READING

3

IDEOLOGICAL BOUNDARIES OF THE IMMIGRATION DEBATE

Ronald Brownstein

Ronald Brownstein wrote the following statement for the Los Angeles Times. *He summarizes the competing political theories that try to explain the global problems of legal and illegal immigration.*

■ **POINTS TO CONSIDER**

1. Explain the difference between restrictionists and advocates of open immigration.

2. What is causing illegal immigration?

3. How is immigration a global problem?

4. Summarize the relationship between the Mexican economy and illegal immigration.

Ronald Brownstein, "Immigration Debate Heats Up," **Los Angeles Times**, December 2, 1993. Copyright, 1993 Los Angeles Times. Reprinted by permission.

The issues raised by immigration – especially illegal immigration – may be fundamentally resistant to long-term "solution."

The search for solutions to the complex and vexing problems of immigration is rapidly polarizing along ideological lines. In the clash of proliferating legislative proposals, diametric views are contending for control of the immigration debate.

On one side are restrictionists, most of them political conservatives, who want to combat illegal immigration by bolstering the U.S. Border Patrol, creating a new form of national identification card and slashing access to government benefits. Many want to reduce the level of legal immigration as well.

On the other side are advocates of relatively open immigration, most of them liberals, who want to protect the current level of legal immigration and shift the focus from punishing illegal immigrants to taking sanctions against the employers who hire them.

FIREWORKS

The intense polarization between these viewpoints guarantees legislative fireworks. It also diminishes the prospects that policymakers will reach consensus on new initiatives – and, even if they do, that those measures will be far-reaching enough to ameliorate the public anxieties over immigration. "It will be very difficult to act," said Frank Sharry, executive director of the National Immigration Forum, an immigrant rights group based in Washington. "When you get down to the actual policymaking...these are very complex issues that don't lend themselves to easy solutions."

LEGAL VS ILLEGAL

On legal immigration, the dispute is fundamental. Restrictionists such as Sen. Harry Reid, D-NV, are pushing for a sharp reversal of the quarter-century trend toward increased legal immigration. They maintain that the country cannot socially or economically absorb the 700,000 legal newcomers a year sanctioned under current law. But President Clinton and other immigration advocates defend high levels of legal immigration as a reflection of fundamental U.S. values.

On illegal immigration, the differences between the camps derive from contradictory diagnoses of the problem. Most restrictionists say that "magnets" draw illegal immigrants to the United States. Thus they focus on making it more arduous to cross the border and more difficult for illegal immigrants to acquire jobs and government benefits once they arrive. "We should not have contradictory policies that undermine the effort to try to control the border," said California Gov. Pete Wilson. "We are inviting, enticing, providing an incentive to illegal immigration by providing services."

Even supporters of relatively open immigration increasingly acknowledge the need for greater enforcement along the border. But they reject the contention that government benefits draw illegal migrants to the United States. They condemn proposals to deny the limited benefits available to illegal immigrants as not only inhumane but ineffective. Rather, many argue, government should hire more inspectors to enforce existing wage, hour and safety laws, compelling employers to clean up working conditions and stop wage violations that make some jobs now more attractive to illegal immigrants than to citizens.

A GLOBAL PROBLEM

You have to address the fact that we have jobs where people will be forced to work for less than the minimum wage in terrible working conditions, and as a result you have a lot of Americans who will resist those conditions," said Rep. Xavier Becerra, D-CA. "If we did a much better job of enforcing existing law, you would make it more attractive for U.S. citizens and lawful residents to take some of those jobs."

To many experts, both sides of this debate are overselling the potential impact of their remedies. The issues raised by immigration – especially illegal immigration – may be fundamentally resistant to long-term "solution." Around the world, experts say, developed countries will inexorably face more pressure for migration from rapidly growing populations in the Third World seeking economic opportunity, particularly when wide wage disparities beckon across open borders, as in the United States and Mexico. In such circumstances, many analysts maintain, the most realistic goal is to control the flow of illegal immigration, not eliminate it.

"It's not an issue that can be solved, unless some very dramatic things change in the world," said Doris Meissner, commissioner of

> # THE INDIANS AT PLYMOUTH ROCK DID NOT DEPORT THE BRITISH
>
> "All of our people – except full-blooded Indians – are immigrants, or descendants of immigrants, including even those who came here on the Mayflower."
>
> "We are a nation of many nationalities, many races, many religions – bound together by a single unity, the unity of freedom and equality. Whoever seeks to set one nationality against another seeks to degrade all nationalities."
>
> *— Franklin D. Roosevelt*

the Immigration and Naturalization Service. "We're talking about a new global reality that we have to find ways of living with and managing and not somehow delude ourselves into thinking that we can make it go away."

CONGRESS

At the top of the agenda for Congress are proposals to tighten control of the national borders. The Clinton administration entered the debate with proposals to reform the system for granting asylum to those claiming political persecution. As Congress grapples with the issue, the key decision will be how to protect legitimate claims while intensifying efforts to weed out those that are fraudulent.

Larger issues are looming. From the administration and legislators in both parties, proposals are proliferating to increase staffing for the Border Patrol and to modernize its equipment.

In both parties, there is a widespread sense that the 1986 immigration reform law has failed to discourage employers from hiring illegal immigrants, largely because it failed to limit the availability of counterfeit documents employees can use to demonstrate legal status. That consensus is reviving broad interest in the creation of a "tamper-proof" form of national identification card that would be required for employment. The White House is studying the issue, and calls for the creation of such a card are a centerpiece of all major Republican immigration proposals. But many groups supporting immigrant rights oppose the notion, maintaining that such a card will lead to discrimination against minorities.

However, to Wayne Cornelius, an expert on U.S.-Mexican relations at the University of California at San Diego, those seeking to deter illegal immigration by fortifying the border and sweeping the work places are focusing on the wrong end of the equation. "There is a pretty strong consensus among immigration specialists," he said, "that a developmental approach focused on the sending countries is the only thing likely to have a long-term deterrent effect on immigration." Thus, Cornelius maintained, the recently approved North American Free Trade Agreement (NAFTA) offers the best hope of reducing the flow of illegal migrants from Mexico; after the agreement has been in place for a decade, illegal immigration from Mexico should drop by more than half, he projected.

MEXICAN ECONOMY

Almost everyone in the immigration debate agrees that any long-term program to control illegal immigration requires invigorating Mexico's economy. But not everyone is as sanguine as Cornelius. For one thing, many experts – Cornelius included – expect NAFTA to increase immigration pressures over the near term, as small and medium-sized Mexican companies face increased competition from the United States.

Over the foreseeable future, then, it's unlikely that Mexican economic development alone will substantially alleviate the pressure on officials to deal with illegal immigration. But the polarized nature of the debate argues against quick consensus on new directions.

HISTORY

History buttresses those predicting delay. Major shifts in immigration policy usually require many years of debate and disagreement before consensus emerges. The employer sanctions approved as part of the 1986 federal law on illegal immigration, for instance, had been debated since the early 1950s.

But the intensity of public uneasiness over immigration gusts in the other direction. "We are in the midst of the first grass-roots immigration debate in 100 years," said Daniel Stein, executive director of the Federation for American Immigration Reform, a group that wants to reduce immigration.

WHAT IS EDITORIAL BIAS?

This activity may be used as an individualized study guide for students in libraries and resource centers or as a discussion catalyst in small group and classroom discussions.

The capacity to recognize an author's point of view is an essential reading skill. The skill to read with insight and understanding involves the ability to detect different kinds of opinions or bias. **Sex bias, race bias, ethnocentric bias, political bias,** and **religious bias** are five basic kinds of opinions expressed in editorials and all literature that attempts to persuade. They are briefly defined below.

Five Kinds of Editorial Opinion or Bias

- **Sex Bias** – The expression of dislike for and/or feeling of superiority over the opposite sex or a particular sexual minority.

- **Race Bias** – The expression of dislike for and/or feeling of superiority over a racial group.

- **Ethnocentric Bias** – The expression of a belief that one's own group, race, religion, culture, or nation is superior. Ethnocentric persons judge others by their own standards and values.

- **Political Bias** – The expression of political opinions and attitudes about domestic or foreign affairs.

- **Religious Bias** – The expression of a religious belief or attitude.

Guidelines

1. From the readings in Chapter One, locate five sentences that provide examples of editorial opinion or bias.

2. Write down the above sentences and determine what kind of bias each sentence represents. Is it **sex bias, race bias, ethnocentric bias, political bias,** or **religious bias?**

3. Make up a one-sentence statement that would be an example of each of the following: **sex bias, race bias, ethnocentric bias, political bias,** and **religious bias.**

4. See if you can locate five sentences that are factual statements from the readings in Chapter One.

CHAPTER 2

RETHINKING THE UNIVERSAL NATION

READING

4

A MORATORIUM ON IMMIGRATION

Dan Stein

Dan Stein is the Executive Director of the Federation for American Immigration Reform (FAIR). FAIR is a national public interest organization working to restrict the current level of legal and illegal immigration. The following comments came before a congressional hearing on immigration legislation.

■ POINTS TO CONSIDER

1. How is the general public's attitude toward immigration portrayed?

2. What is the relationship between population growth and immigration?

3. Explain the changes taking place between urban and rural populations inside poor nations of the world.

4. Dan Stein defines an urgent mission for the U.S. Explain this mission.

5. What steps can be taken to end illegal immigration?

6. Summarize the nature of the worker verification system advocated by the author.

Excerpted from congressional testimony by Dan Stein before the House Judiciary Committee, June 29, 1995.

We have the moral right to limit immigration, or indeed to stop all immigration entirely.

Elections, polls and other indicators reveal that the general public is more than ready for a moratorium on immigration. Poll after poll reveals that an overwhelming majority of the American people favor reduced immigration or an overall "time out" until we get our own house in order. Moreover, the results from last year's election, particularly the resounding victory of California's Proposition 187, reflect a society-wide sentiment in favor of broad, deep reductions in immigration and an improved capacity for overall immigration law enforcement.

There are several points in the destiny of a great nation where the ship changes course dramatically. It is a time when an old policy is abandoned, and a new one is adopted, taking the nation toward an entirely new direction. The public is ready, and the process is in place, for major and significant strides toward new and exciting changes – changes that will make immigration again serve the national interests.

Federation for American Immigration Reform (FAIR) has been working to secure meaningful immigration reform for many years. We are well aware of the political challenges represented by such an emotional and delicate task. For that reason, we doubly applaud your leadership.

GROWING BORDER PRESSURES

America's greatest security threat is not a ballistic missile. It is our inability to regulate our borders. Never before have so many people wanted to move to the United States. A recent Gallup poll of public opinion worldwide found that, conservatively, perhaps half a billion people will readily admit they want to move to the United States – now, today. In some countries, perhaps 25 percent of the entire urban population wants to move to the U.S. Given that we are in the midst of the greatest surge of world population growth in the history of the human race, and that these rapid increases are the single most important reason for the ever-increasing numbers of people trying to come to the U.S. legally and illegally, we must act with speed and deliberation to improve our entry controls and establish more enforceable immigration laws.

In several publications, FAIR has sought to highlight the specific dimensions of this phenomenon. In doing so, we have sought to highlight three points: 1) Rapid population growth is placing untenable immigration pressures on the United States. 2) Immigration and U.S. population growth patterns generally are regionally-concentrated, especially in coastal counties. This coastal county growth has far-reaching consequences that affect other parts of the nation and even the rest of the world. 3) Given population and natural resource/environmental pressures, there are now profound, urgent reasons to address immigration within a broader, national population policy framework.

The United Nations estimates that 90 million people are now added to the population of the world each year. In just the next ten years, more people will be added to the population than there were in the entire world in the year 1800. Just two generations ago, total world population was 2.5 billion. And that was considered a remarkable number. In 1992, we reached the 5.5 billion mark, and the UN estimates that we will exceed 10 billion in the next century before population levels off.

This demographic force will generate an unprecedented wave of human migration in the 21st Century as tens of millions daily seek economic opportunity, escape from environmental disaster, civil strife and repression. The patterns have just begun to emerge and will grow with intensity in decades to come.

THE POOR NATIONS

In much of the less developed world, we have witnessed the flight from rural to urban areas of the past two generations. Those in the countryside are moving – voting with their feet – in response to poor and declining living conditions. Pushed from the countryside and pulled by the city's bright lights and economic opportunity – real or imagined – tens of millions have elected to crowd into teeming metropolitan areas. Mexico City, for example, with 3.5 million people as recently as 1950, now holds around 18 million. The UN estimates that between 1987 and 2025, the urban population of the Third World will have grown by 2.75 billion – twice the number that were added during the period from 1950 to 1987. In 1950, North America had an urban population of 198 million; Asian (excluding Japan) had an urban population of 175 million. In 1990, the figures were 207 million and 900 million, respectively. By 2025, North America is projected to have 280 million urban dwellers, while Asia will have an

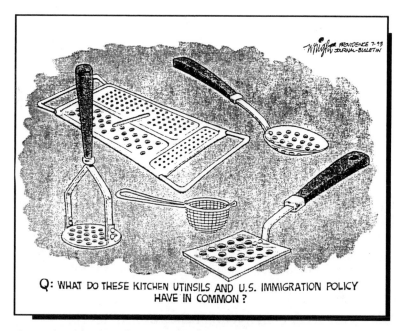

Q: WHAT DO THESE KITCHEN UTINSILS AND U.S. IMMIGRATION POLICY HAVE IN COMMON ?

Cartoon by Richard Wright. Reprinted with permission.

urban population of 2.5 billion – roughly the population of the entire world in 1950.

In other words, by 2025, Asia's urban population will be as large – in itself – as was the population of the entire world in 1950.

In 1990, the entire labor force of the more developed regions was 584 million people. In just the next ten years, the less developed countries will have to produce 372 million jobs to accommodate all the new labor force entrants. These are not projections. The job seekers of the early 21st Century are already born. By 2025, another billion people will be seeking employment, a number more than double the present total labor force of the more developed regions.

These figures represent an economic challenge unsurpassed in the history of the human race. They paint a picture of tomorrow's urban sprawl, or megacity: teeming with uneducated souls, trapped in urban squalor and poverty, who, staring at U.S.-made movies, believe that passage to the United States is the only real opportunity for an improved state of being.

A NATIONAL DEBATE

Let us accept, therefore, that the demand to enter far exceeds our capacity as a nation to accommodate: The age of mass migration is over, and nearly all people must "bloom where they're planted."

To that end, we here in the United States have an urgent mission: We need a national debate that underscores the realities mentioned above, and reconsiders the role of immigration in our national future. We must reassert control over our national policy, and render our immigration and deportation laws enforceable. To achieve that, at a minimum, we need to reduce the backlogs and pressure for growth within the system. We need a moratorium to reduce the volume flowing through the system, and a breather to restructure the current laws to make them more responsive to the national interest. We need to understand why we need immigration in the next century, or if we need it at all.

TEN STEPS TO ENDING ILLEGAL IMMIGRATION

FAIR published a new report entitled "Ten Steps to Ending Illegal Immigration." The report follows a 1989 report by FAIR entitled "Ten Steps to Securing America's Borders," and broadens substantially our analysis of what is needed to truly control illegal immigration. The new report addresses the major subject areas with one hundred specific recommendations that must be addressed by Congress and the Executive Branch if effective entry controls are ever to be re-established.

Our report found that illegal immigration cannot be controlled solely at the border. Stacking agents along the border – or relocating all Immigration and Naturalization Service (INS) and Border Patrol personnel to the high-volume crossing point in San Diego – will not work. Rather, the only effective method of controlling the problem is to deploy a balanced approach that involves a full range of enforcement improvements. These include many legislative, procedural and processing reforms, beefed up investigations capacity, asylum reform, documents improvements, dramatic improvements to the efficiency of INS detention and deportation, limitations on judicial review, improved intelligence capacity, better state/federal cooperation, and new funding sources. Curtailing unlawful migration also means ensuring that persons who enter illegally or through fraud will not be able to obtain unauthorized employment, welfare, education, housing, and other societal benefits without detection. To achieve this, INS must become a key player in assisting state, local and private agencies in the verification of citizenship or alienage status at key intervention points (employment and benefits application, for example).

RESTRICTIONS AGAINST EMPLOYMENT

Until 1986, there was no specific ban on the knowing employment of illegal aliens. That loophole was a powerful invitation to the unemployed in other countries to illegally enter the United States. The Immigration Reform and Control Act of 1986 (IRCA) made such hiring, under certain circumstances, a crime, imposing an escalating series of civil and criminal penalties against those who knowingly hired illegal workers. The message of the new law spread quickly to other lands; illegal crossings plummeted the first three years as foreigners realized that the primary incentive to violate U.S. immigration laws – U.S. jobs – had been eliminated.

By 1989, a thriving cottage industry in phony documents had developed that illegal aliens used to skirt the new law. That message also reached other lands, and illegal crossings are again on the rise. A Department of Justice and INS report, *"Immigration Reform and Control Act: Report on Legalized Population"* (March 1992), stated that 83% of the aliens amnestied under the 1990 Immigration Reform Act had false social security cards.

There is a great deal of public support for a uniform, secure work verification system. In polls conducted in June 1990 and

April 1991 by the Roper Organization, concerning "American Attitudes Toward Immigration," over 60% of those questioned stated that they favored a government-issued, forge-proof, easily verifiable identification document that would have to be shown only when applying for a job. Recent polls also demonstrate that legal immigrants themselves support a secure work verification system; they have more than anyone to gain from such a system. We believe the public is ready for a bolder initiative to implement an electronic verification of employment and benefits eligibility system nationwide:

ELIGIBILITY CONFIRMATION PROCESS

In 1986, Congress provided an IRCA authorization for the President to request the Attorney General to test telephone verification as an alternative to the actual presentation of documents to an employer during hiring transactions. Patterned after credit card systems, such a system would enable employers to transmit a number electronically, perhaps the social security number, to receive verification of work eligibility.

The Honorable Barbara Jordan, Chair of the Commission on Immigration Reform, stated in testimony on August 3, 1994, before the Senate Subcommittee on Immigration and Refugee Affairs that the "Commission believes that the most promising option for more secure, non-discriminatory verification is a computerized registry, using data provided by the Social Security Administration (SSA) and the Immigration and Naturalization Service." The key to which is the Social Security number. All workers must have a number before accepting work. FAIR agrees with the Commissioner that only one document, probably a variant of the current Social Security card, should be used to prove worker (and benefits) eligibility.

Under IRCA, the nation's estimated 7 million employers are required to review a variety of documents allowed as evidence of identity and employment eligibility. Most employers, however, are not in a position to make sound judgments on the genuineness of these documents. Indeed, employers have been given little guidance and education on the characteristics of fraudulent and genuine documents. Moreover, even SSA employees, who are trained in document authentication, often have difficulty determining whether documents are authentic and relate to the person presenting them.

SOCIAL SECURITY CARD

To improve employer verification, the Social Security card should be designated as the only authorized employment eligibility document. The General Accounting Office (GAO) has said this for years. It has recommended the use of the Social Security card as the single document that should be used as evidence of employment eligibility under IRCA. In a March 1988 report, the GAO states that, "We believe that the Social Security card would meet the needs of both employers and employees and offer advantages over the present system. With such a change employers would have only the Social Security card with which to become familiar, rather than the thousands of different birth certificates and other documents that now can be provided as evidence of employment eligibility. Also, educating employers in detecting fraudulent cards would be more feasible than trying to educate them on the many types of documents now authorized."

CONCLUSION

In order to make immigration reform a reality, the special interest groups that have, for years, dominated the process and dictated the results will have to be overcome. We will work hard to try to insure that all Americans understand the importance of this legislation.

READING

THE CASE FOR OPEN IMMIGRATION

Jane Guskin

Jane Guskin works with the Weekly News Update on the Americas. *For a free one-month trial subscription, write the Nicaragua Solidarity Network at 339 Lafayette Street, New York, NY 10012; (212) 674-9499; email: nicanet%transfr@blythe.org.*

■ POINTS TO CONSIDER

1. How have immigrants been discriminated against in American history?

2. What is the relationship between cheap labor and free trade?

3. Why did NAFTA work to the disadvantage of labor and many immigrants?

4. Analyze the relationship that the author sees between population and immigration.

5. Why do immigrants face an unfair tax burden?

6. Describe the relationship between increasing border violence against immigrants and greater security measures to prevent border crossings by illegals.

Jane Guskin, "Whose Land?" **The Nonviolent Activist**, June, 1994. Adapted from an article originally published in **The Nonviolent Activist**, the magazine of the War Resisters League, a national pacifist organization founded in 1923 and located at 339 Lafayette St., New York, NY 10012; (212) 228-0450; email wrl@igc.apc.org.

It is once again up to activists to refute the standard arguments for restrictive immigration policies.

Since the beginning of time, people have moved across lands, oceans and continents in search of a better life. Here in the United States of America, which everyone agrees was built by immigrants, we are now being told that we've had enough. There's no more room, no more jobs, no more food. We can't afford to let any more of "them" into "our" country. Any argument against the new xenophobia – we are an immigrant nation, after all – is dismissed with "that was the past. Things are different now." But those old enough to remember will find the new arguments hauntingly familiar; they have been used for over a century to tighten border controls and scapegoat immigrants whenever the economy gets bad.

Economic, political and military violence inflicted on poor countries by wealthy nations comes full circle when those individuals trying to escape the resultant poverty and oppression are attacked physically and economically at and within First World borders.

I'M OK, YOU'RE NOT

As early as May 1844, Protestants in Philadelphia destroyed the homes of Irish immigrants and attacked a Catholic church, claiming unskilled Irish workers were taking jobs from skilled native workers. Legal restrictions on immigration to the U.S. began with the Chinese Exclusion Act of 1882, spurred by protests in California against Chinese workers. During the great immigration wave of the 1890s, Samuel Gompers of the American Federation of Labor – himself a Dutch-born Jewish immigrant from England – complained that the recent arrivals of the time consisted of "cheap labor, ignorant labor that takes our jobs and cuts our wages."

Anti-immigrant sentiment grew, and little by little, curbs were imposed on the newcomers – first on those with contagious diseases or serious criminal records, then on those who were "professional beggars," anarchists, prostitutes or epileptics. A 1910 Congressional report on the immigration "problem" declared that the miserable living conditions in immigrant ghettos in major U.S. cities were caused by "inherent racial tendencies," rather than poverty. And in 1924, Congress passed the Johnson-Reed Act, which placed a cap on overall immigration from outside the

Western Hemisphere, divided into quotas based on nationality. Asians were completely excluded.

Quotas based on national origin, eliminated in 1965, returned in the 1980s and are growing more restrictive with each new immigration policy. Our government now also excludes people who are HIV-positive or have AIDS from entering the U.S., and all those seeking legal residence here are required to take an HIV test. Anti-immigrant sentiment among the U.S. public – heavily promoted by the mainstream media – is growing again, with most of the fury directed against undocumented immigrants...

CALIFORNIA

In California the tension is at a high, with extended earthquake relief being denied to those without documents. California Governor Pete Wilson has proposed eliminating prenatal care assistance for undocumented pregnant women and denying citizenship and public education to the children of undocumented immigrants. California and other state governments (New Jersey, New York, Texas and Florida, for example) are now demanding that the federal government reimburse them for their "unfair burden" of services to undocumented immigrants.

As the pressure increases, it is once again up to archivists to refute the standard arguments for restrictive immigration policies – that immigrants take jobs away from native-born workers, bring down overall wage levels, create congestion and overpopulation, and place an unfair burden on certain communities or on the nation as a whole by using more in services than they contribute in taxes – and to push for an opening of our borders.

CHEAP LABOR, FREE TRADE

Many refute the contention that new immigrants take low-wage unskilled jobs away from U.S. citizens by arguing that most U.S. citizens don't want these jobs anyway. The simple fact is that under our capitalist system, bosses will always exploit their workers as much as they can for the least amount of pay. It is California's large farm owners, for example, who have the most to gain from illegal immigration – not the immigrant workers themselves, who end up with cancer and birth defects from pesticides sprayed on the fields where they work long, arduous days for little pay. No one – not immigrants, not citizens – should have to work

40

Cartoon by Steve Kelly. Reprinted with permission of **Coply News Service**.

these jobs as long as they are dangerous, unfairly compensated and oppressive.

It should be clear to everyone by now that if employers cannot find workers in this country who they can easily exploit for the maximum profit, they will move elsewhere. The North American Free Trade Agreement (NAFTA) simply clinches the deal by tearing down national borders for large corporations while maintaining them for workers. Other regional trade agreements – like the European Economic Community and the Central American trade pact, for example – provide for the free movement of capital and labor, meaning that workers from any one of the countries involved can legally work in any of the others. NAFTA pointedly excludes workers from the new trade "freedom."

If undocumented immigrants drive down wages, this is not because they are immigrants but because they are undocumented, and their fear of deportation makes them easier to exploit. If they could work here legally, they could demand the same rights – and the same wages – as everyone else. Actually, undocumented immigrants are entitled to the same rights, and courts have supported these rights in cases involving labor disputes. But most people don't know what their rights are, and certainly not how to fight for them.

Only more effective labor organizing can reverse the downward trend of wages in this country. And organizers from the United Electrical (UE) and Service Employees (SEIU) unions have discovered that in fact many immigrants bring a new militancy to labor struggles. Workers in California who organized with UE drew on their experiences from Mexico and Central America, using tactics such as hunger strikes and tent encampments to win their fight against a computer manufacturer. "Even striking over the firing of another worker is a reflection of our culture of mutual support, which workers bring with them to this country," points out Maria Pantoja, a UE organizer and Mexico City native, in an article in *Third Force* magazine. And while immigrant workers are more vulnerable to employer retaliation, SEIU leader Eliseo Medina explains that "when you come from a country where they shoot you for being a unionist or a striker, then getting fired from your job doesn't seem so bad."

Another tragedy often ignored is the waste of talent caused by immigration restrictions. Many undocumented immigrants are doctors, nurses, lawyers, accountants, teachers and other skilled professionals, with training and experience from their countries of origin. Unable to get jobs in their field because they are "illegal," many survive by selling flowers or shish kabobs on the street, looking after someone else's children, cleaning out vats of toxic chemicals in factories, picking fruit, washing dishes, mopping floors or removing asbestos.

CONGESTION AND OVERPOPULATION

Whether or not you think overpopulation is a problem, closing borders does not address the real issue. It is at best a temporary band-aid for the wealthy to continue their inexcusable waste of the world's resources. It is at face value an unjust and indefensible method of avoiding our own complicity in the population equation and therefore not actually dealing with the problem. Many population theorists argue that while population is indeed a grave issue, it is a global one, and one that should not be addressed with repressive measures but by attacking root causes such as inequitable distribution of wealth and lack of women's rights. Studies have shown, for example, that as women gain greater self-determination and control over their lives (through such means as education, employment, land ownership, decision-making, and access to contraceptives and safe abortions) the birth rate declines significantly.

The congestion argument is just as easily dismissed. Much of this country's population shift into the cities has been internal: as small farming disappears and automation increases, farming jobs vanish and workers are forced out of rural areas into the cities. Immigrants, like native workers, will go where the jobs are. They can hardly be blamed for our government's failure to support family farmers.

UNFAIR TAX BURDEN?

In reality, immigrants pay about $90 billion a year in federal, state and local taxes. But they only get about $5 billion a year in social services. In fact, the average immigrant family pays about $2,500 more in taxes each year than it receives in tax-supported benefits of all kinds.

Everyone – documented, undocumented or citizen – pays sales tax. While many undocumented immigrants work under-the-table jobs and do not contribute payroll taxes, many do – by using false social security numbers. These taxpayers may even be due refunds, but cannot collect them with a false social security number. In addition, most undocumented immigrants, fearful of deportation, do not seek social benefits that may be due them.

As a matter of fact, all of us are putting in more taxes than we receive in services – unless you count pumping up the military

43

budget and bailing out the savings and loan disaster as services. If we really want to get rid of our unfair tax burdens, that's where we should start.

THE BORDER PATROL: INSTITUTIONALIZED VIOLENCE

Some of the links between violence and immigration restrictions are subtle and complicated. More blatant has been the increase in physical violence against new immigrants that accompanies recent legislative and media attacks on newcomers. The American Friends Service Committee has documented a "sharp rise in the level of violent beatings" of Mexican people near the border. The border agents themselves often play a major role in this violence. In 1992, U.S. border patrol agent Michael Elmer shot Mexican national Dario Miranda twice in the back as Miranda was running away. Elmer and another agent hid the body, and Elmer then went to a party. He never reported the incident. At his trial, Elmer pleaded self-defense. A state jury acquitted him of all criminal charges, and a federal jury cleared him of violating Miranda's civil rights.

Knowing they cannot stop the flow of immigration, agents see the back-and-forth chase across the border as a game. "At first I used to get really frustrated," one border patrol agent told a *New York Times* reporter. "Now I just try to have as much fun as I can."... Most ironic of all is that all the border states once belonged to Mexico, and if anyone, besides indigenous people, has a right to live in them, it should be Mexicans.

POLITICAL ASYLUM: THE VIOLENCE OF EXCLUSION

Our policies on political asylum inflict further violence on immigrants. While our government officially acknowledges that Haiti's current military regime is repressive and has murdered thousands, those who flee it are stopped on the high seas by the U.S. Coast Guard and shipped back to be fingerprinted and photographed by the same forces they are fleeing. And while U.S. officials privately acknowledge that the vast majority of Cubans who leave the island are fleeing economic hard times, these "refugees" are rescued, welcomed like heroes and – thanks to a special law created just for Cubans who arrive illegally – given green cards automatically after they have been in the U.S. a year and a day. When refugees die trying to get into our country, the media focuses on the "traffickers" who bring them, rather than on our own government for encouraging their illegal journeys by preventing their legal entry.

The Refugee Act authorizes political asylum to anyone who demonstrates "a well-founded fear of persecution on account of race, religion, nationality, membership in a particular social group, or political opinion." But application of these guidelines grows stricter each year. People fleeing forced military service by either government or rebel armies do not qualify...

SHUT IN, SHUT OUT: THE "ILLEGALS"

"Illegal" immigrants often find themselves trapped: cut off from friends and relatives, unable to travel, and unable to find a better job or a better life. They remain prisoners inside our borders. Most would have preferred to remain in their homeland if there was a chance at a decent life there. Their flight from war-torn nations and ravaged economies is a direct result of U.S. military aid to repressive regimes; a direct result of the ever-expanding arms trade, which seeks to foment regional conflicts into new markets for its products; a direct result of the "neoliberal" economic measures forced on poor nations by the International Monetary Fund, which causes desperate poverty (and the reappearance in epidemic proportions of diseases like cholera and tuberculosis) through massive cutbacks in social services, layoffs, and privatization.

Our struggle against the violence that causes this immigration must first address our own government's complicity in it. At the same time we must provide a safe haven for those suffering its effects.

READING

6

ALIEN NATION: THE POINT

Joseph A. Varacalli

Joseph A. Varacalli teaches sociology at Nassau Community College.

■ POINTS TO CONSIDER

1. Why is immigration described as out of control?

2. Define what the author means by the phrase "new class multicultural elites."

3. Describe the "four important differences between the turn-of-the-last-century immigration and our equally impressive contemporary one."

4. Why is a moratorium on immigration needed?

Joseph A. Varacalli, "Divided We Fall," **Crisis:** Washington, DC, Nov. 95. Reprinted by permission.

Immigration cannot be defended on the utilitarian grounds of meeting the needs of the American economy or nation.

Reading *Alien Nation*, I could not help but notice the kind of folks that author Peter Brimelow has attracted to his anti-immigrant cause: old-guard WASPs, population controllers, hard-core-environmentalists, and nativists of all stripes. These are, to put it mildly, among the last kind of people I'd like to get stuck with in an elevator. But Mr. Brimelow's impressive treatise deserves to stand or fall on its own merits as a depiction of present reality and as a projection of the American future.

NO CONTROL

Brimelow claims many things. For one, he argues that immigration – both legal and illegal – presently is out of control, a direct result of a tragic, irrational, and misconceived 1965 Immigration Act along with its subsequent amendments. Combined with the present white birth dearth, massive Third World immigration is fast pushing America into an unprecedented and tumultuous period of racial and ethnic transformation. Her original Northwestern European foundations are being left far behind. Second, Brimelow calculates that immigration is not economically necessary for the American nation and not beneficial when the economy is high tech and the immigrants aren't. He asserts that contemporary immigrants, compared with the native population, are disproportionately under-skilled, under-educated, hard to assimilate, crime-prone, disease carriers, susceptible to welfare dependency and to the creation of non-indigenous underclasses.

NEW CLASS ELITES

For Brimelow, then, immigration cannot be defended on the utilitarian grounds of meeting the needs of the American economy or nation. Nor is it a civil right. Nor is it a matter of historical destiny. It is the result of a quite reversible social policy. Very importantly, however, he holds that the motivation for opening up the floodgates since 1965 is not solely or even primarily altruistic in nature. Rather, he claims that the motivation takes root in the psychological and political needs of "alienists," that is, the anti-American new class. Borrowing an argument from the neo-conservative play book, he calculates that the overthrow of white,

47

Protestant America will provide much emotional satisfaction to new class multicultural elites, who are either non-WASPs, screaming and pushing their way to the top, or traitors to their own class. Indeed, Brimelow foresees the grim possibility, in the not-too-distant future, of nothing less than the balkanization and dissolution of the United States of America.

FOUR DIFFERENCES

It is not quite fair to state, as pro-immigrationists want to do, that Brimelow's anti-immigration arguments have all been heard before and that the sky didn't fall and isn't falling. Brimelow claims that there are four important differences between the massive turn-of-the-last-century immigration and our equally impressive contemporary one. First, today's immigrants are mostly from the Third World and, therefore, not capable of assimilating easily into America's basic Northwestern European heritage. Second, immigrants are not urged by our present-day cultural elite to assimilate as were prior foreigners. Third, unlike in the past, there is a massive welfare state that leads immigrants into dependency; failed immigrants today stay, Brimelow argues, and do not go back from whence they came. And, fourth, earlier immigration was consciously stopped to allow for the digestion of Catholics, Orthodox Christians, and Jews; at present there is no sign of an impending lull.

SOCIAL INSTITUTIONS

Playing devil's advocate, let me add to Brimelow's list a fifth argument: our social institutions (or potential "mediating structures") are in no shape to help absorb a massive influx of immigrants given the demonstrated failure of these institutions to meet intellectual, moral, and practical needs of America's native population. As a Catholic who enthusiastically accepts his religion's stated mission to evangelize, the introduction of millions of Third-Worlders to this country theoretically provides a wonderful opportunity to spread the faith and, derivatively, strengthen America by mooring her better on Catholic principles. Empirically, however, the present leadership of the Catholic Church in America can't even teach middle-class kids the Ten Commandments, never mind leading Third-Worlders into the warm waters of the faith. Moreover, the failure of the American Catholic hierarchy to evangelize successfully among Hispanic immigrants is nothing less

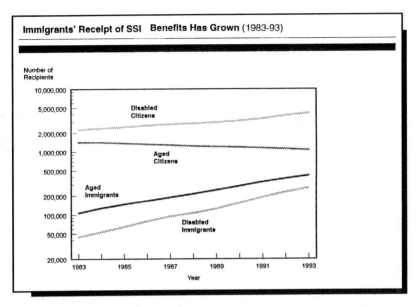

Immigrants' Receipt of SSI Benefits Has Grown (1983-93)

Source: Social Security Administration

than scandalous and is indicative of a basically bankrupt institution. Likewise, following Brimelow's logic, what is the purpose of exposing immigrant children to an educational system corrupted by Marxists, feminists, and their ilk? Brimelow, in this regard, notes the overt racial hostility towards whites exhibited by significant sectors of the contemporary Puerto Rican community.

MULTICULTURALISTS

The eminent sociologist Peter L. Berger may be right when he stresses that the problem is with the multiculturalists and not with the immigrants. The latter, in the main, fully accept the culture of middle-America, which essentially reads, following George Gilder, "work, family, and faith breeds a successful life." Put another way, the assumption is that the average contemporary immigrant rejects both cultural end-poles of American life, the degeneracies of both underclass and, more culpably, new class life.

The problem, however, is that there is also some fragmentary evidence of immigrant students being co-opted by the multiculturalists that control so many contemporary educational institutions. Is this evidence a harbinger of things to come? Under sustained

49

RECOMMENDATIONS

Brimelow himself is blunt about the political course he would have the nation follow. Here are some of his recommendations:

- Double the size of the Border Patrol.

- "Urgently" increase the size of the Immigration and Naturalization Service.

- Institute a new "Operation Wetback" to expel illegal aliens.

- If necessary, establish a national identity card.

- Go beyond employer sanctions to the interdiction of money transfers by illegals to their home countries.

- Make it clear that there will never again be an amnesty for illegal immigrants.

- Discontinue immigration for the purposes of family reunification. If family reunification is permitted at all, confine it to the nuclear family.

- Move the INS from the Justice Department to the Labor Department, and make an immigration applicant's skills the criterion for admission.

- Institute an English-language requirement for immigrants.

- Ban immigration from countries that do not permit reciprocal immigration from the United States.

- Cut legal immigration from the current one million or more annually to 400,000...

- Cut back such special categories as "refugee" and "asylee."

- See to it that no immigrant is eligible for preferential hiring, set-aside college admission, or other forms of affirmative action.

Jack Miles, "The Coming Immigration Debate," **Atlantic Monthly**, Apr., 1995.

multicultural tutelage, will immigrant students eventually become as alienated, angry, and "demanding of their rights" as have some other sectors of America's college population?

MORATORIUM

I am thus forced to take seriously Brimelow's call for a brief moratorium and a thorough and fair national debate about immigration. It is a debate that, thus far, cuts across ideological lines as neo-conservatives and neo-liberals have willingly joined forces against the bizzare coupling of a Ralph Nader with a Ross Perot and a Eugene McCarthy with a Pat Buchanan. Brimelow is right on target when he aims at the elitist bypass that ignores the views on immigration of a concerned citizenry. In sum, let me suggest the following advice: buy *Alien Nation*, and join the national debate.

READING

7

ALIEN NATION: THE COUNTERPOINT

John J. Miller

John J. Miller is vice president of the Center for Equal Opportunity in Washington, D.C. He recently compiled The Index of Leading Immigration Indicators.

■ POINTS TO CONSIDER

1. Who is Peter Brimelow?

2. How do immigrants harm American culture?

3. Why is Brimelow accused of creating a "racist vision"?

4. Where do immigrants come from?

5. What is meant by the term "majority-minority" nation?

John J. Miller, "Wretched Refuse," **Reason**, June, 1995. Reprinted, with permission, from the June 1995 issue of **Reason Magazine**. Copyright 1995 by the Reason Foundation, 3415 S. Sepulveda Blvd., Suite 400, Los Angeles, CA 90034.

Immigration to the United States has been "a triumphant success."

Peter Brimelow never comes right out and says it, but he clearly thinks that immigrants threaten America's future more than southern secession, the Great Depression, or the Cold War ever did. "America has never faced a greater challenge," he claims in *Alien Nation*. Indeed, the very first sentence of this scaremongering book outlandishly invokes the image of goosestepping Nazis: "Current immigration policy is Adolf Hitler's posthumous revenge on America," writes Brimelow. He never really explains why this is so, but that's fairly typical for this disappointing book of half-explanations and half-truths.

It had promised to be so much more. As a writer for *Forbes*, Brimelow for years has deservedly earned high marks for his reporting on the environment, regulation, and other issues. His exposés on teacher unions are classic. So when he penned an issue-length essay for *National Review* in 1992 arguing to cut back on immigration, Brimelow was taken very seriously by the free-market conservatives who intuitively oppose such measures. He set off a fierce debate on the right and quickly became a standard-bearer for anti-immigrant forces.

ALIEN NATION

Alien Nation spends so much time blaming so many things on immigrants that it rarely bothers to stop, take a deep breath, and focus on one matter at a time. To Brimelow, just about every aspect of the current wave of immigrants represents an unmitigated tragedy for the United States. Today's newcomers, he argues, fracture American culture. They hurt the environment. They bring diseases. They have the curious habit of both stealing jobs from Americans and going on the dole. Pick a problem – any problem – and somewhere in this book Brimelow will find a way to blame it on immigrants.

This tendentious fault finding pervades *Alien Nation*. Consider, for example, how Brimelow cites the Alexis de Tocqueville Institute's 1990 poll of leading economists. In this survey, 80 percent concluded that the United States has profited from 20th-century immigration and another two-thirds thought that increased immigration would boost U.S. living standards. Brimelow's spin: "Immigration is a subject that much of the American elite gets emotional about" and "economists are part of the elite benefiting at the expense of their fellow Americans." Both of these points may be absolutely true, but they hardly negate the opinions of a group that included James Buchanan, Milton Friedman, and John Kenneth Galbraith.

To engage its topic seriously, *Alien Nation* would have to dispense with its cynicism and deliver a full-blown discussion of the good, bad, and unquantifiable impacts of immigrants on our economy, culture, and society. It never does. Like a kid with a short attention span, it's too eager to rush off for more fun somewhere else. The book's arguments mimic a blunderbuss as they blast scattershot in a dozen different directions at once; most miss their targets entirely or just fizzle into failure...

RACIST VISION

Perhaps the worst thing immigrants do is fuel Brimelow's feverish prose. "The nearest thing to a precedent" for today's influx, he argues, is the 5th-century Roman empire, which was overrun by Vandals, Visigoths, and other assorted villains. Yet we moderns actually have it much worse than the Romans ever did: "The Germans were Western Europeans. They were virtually identical to the populations they conquered and with whom, in most cases, they proceeded quickly to merge." Americans should be so lucky! The dusky hordes of Mexico won't go nearly as easy on us. ("The Huns, by the way, weren't exactly "Western Europeans.")

This sentiment – white barbarian armies aren't as bad as non-white migrants – highlights the unsettling racialist vision underscoring *Alien Nation*. America, says Brimelow, has a "specific ethnic core" of "white" people. What he seems to forget is that this supposed core is actually made up of many ethnicities. They may seem more or less alike today (don't tell my Irish-American father-in-law!), but only by way of a certain historical blindness.

When boatloads of Greek, Italian, and Jewish people arrived on American shores around the turn of the century, they didn't all embrace each other like long-lost cousins. They came from Europe, a place where there are no "whites" – only Bulgarians, Norwegians, Spaniards, Welsh, etc. They viewed themselves as profoundly different from one another, as well as from the largely Anglo native population. Most had very mixed feelings about

assimilation, and they struggled both to cling to their old ways and to adapt in a new land. What their descendants share today is a culture distilled mainly from the British Isles, but with distinctly American peculiarities.

NEWCOMERS

Today's newcomers may seem as strange to us as many of our grandparents did to Woodrow Wilson, who once accused "hyphenated Americans" of divided national loyalties. About 85 percent of immigrants to the United States over the past 25 years have come from nontraditional source countries in Asia, the Caribbean, and Latin America. To Brimelow, this remarkable diversity of people boils down to a simple "Us v. Them" equation. Immigrants from such disparate places as Korea, Haiti, and Guatemala all hail from "one area," namely, the "Third World."

For Brimelow, they are people like Colin Ferguson, the Jamaican-born madman who opened fire on a crowded Long Island Railroad train in 1993. Ferguson is an archetype, argues Brimelow, an immigrant everyman. His "particularly instructive" case raises the question "in any rational mind" of whether it's "really wise to allow the immigration of people who find it so difficult and painful to assimilate into the American majority."

55

Follow that reasoning? It goes something like this: Colin Ferguson is bad. Therefore, all immigrants are bad. There was a time when they weren't all bad, Brimelow admits. "Let's be clear about this: the American experience with immigration has been a triumphant success," he writes. But he's disturbingly clear about something else, too: "Then, immigrants came overwhelmingly from Europe, no matter how different they seemed at the time; now, immigrants are overwhelmingly visible minorities from the Third World."

OLD RHETORIC

This sounds very much like the anti-immigrant rhetoric of roughly 80 years ago, when Southern and Eastern Europeans were also "visible minorities." It doesn't take much effort to track down hysterical quotations from respected public figures panicking over how Hungarians would deracinate America. Many scholars used to split Europeans into three different groups: Nordics (best), Alpines (so-so), and Mediterraneans (wretched). Today we can laugh at this pigeonholing. But these ideas undergird the 1924 National Origins Quota system, which made it very hard for immigrants from anywhere outside Northern Europe to gain admission to the United States. This law essentially shut off the flow of immigrants from Southern and Eastern Europe, whose numbers peaked in 1907. It remained more or less in place until 1965, when racism became unfashionable and Congress over-hauled immigration policy.

DISSOLUTION

As a direct result of these reforms, Brimelow argues, the United States is headed toward "dissolution." If current trends continue, he prophesies, the country will divide into Quebec-like enclaves based on race and ethnicity: "An Anglo-Cuban society like Greater Miami is going to have little in common with an Anglo-black society like San Antonio. These will be communities as different from one another as any in the civilized world. They will verge on being separate nations...."

MAJORITY-MINORITY NATION

Demographers regularly remind us that the United States will become a "majority-minority" nation in the next century. But our

56

concepts of race and ethnicity won't fit for much longer into the
neat little boxes devised by Census bureaucrats. They will
implode under the mounting pressure of Americans claiming
unique combinations of ancestors from places such as Cambodia,
El Salvador, and Senegal. Just as the Croatians, Czechs, and Poles
of the early 1900s eventually broadened our notions of pluralism
and identity, so will today's newcomers. According to a poll
taken last year by the National Conference of Christians and Jews,
many immigrants already feel like they're fitting in. When asked
with which racial or ethnic group they shared most in common,
both Asians and Hispanics picked whites – "the American majority" whose erosion so worries Brimelow.

Complete assimilation might take a couple of generations, it
might seem to stall from time to time, and it will surely come with
plenty of rough spots. But it will happen, just as it always has. By
the time 2050 rolls around, today's furor over immigration will
seem like nothing more than another episode in the long series of
fusses Americans have had over every group of strangers at our
gate. If we're still using terms like "majority-minority," they will
probably mean something entirely different and unexpected.

WHITE HEARTLAND

Instead of grappling with these issues, however, Brimelow fantasizes about "America's white heartland" in the "inter-mountain West" and even "the Pacific Northwest going off with an independent British Columbia and Alberta." His belief that multiracial and multiethnic societies cannot work eventually turns into demands for ending immigration entirely, pleas for restrictionist groups like the Carrying Capacity Network, the Federation for American Immigration Reform, and Negative Population Growth.

We've seen anxieties over immigration come and go before. Brimelow simply trumpets their arrival once again, parroting much of what's been said in the past and occasionally updating it for the 1990s. Even if immigration enthusiasts have not always won their political fights, they can at least take comfort in knowing that history has typically vindicated their thinking. Immigration to the United States has been, to borrow Brimelow's phrase, "a triumphant success." It remains so today. And there's no reason to impose a moratorium on our optimism about it now.

READING

8

ASIAN IMMIGRANTS: THE POINT

Samuel Francis

Samuel Francis is a nationally syndicated columnist and a prominent spokesman for conservative causes and ideas.

■ POINTS TO CONSIDER

1. Why is the positive stereotype of Asian immigrants not an accurate one?

2. Identify congressional actions that Asian Americans are worried about.

3. What is the relationship between immigration and civil rights, according to Asian immigration advocates?

4. According to the author, Asians are organizing as Asians. Why does he call this a form of racial consciousness?

5. Why should "real Americans" oppose mass immigration?

Samuel Francis, "Mass Immigration," **Tribune Media Services, Inc.**, 1996. © **Tribune Media Services**, Inc. Reprinted with permission.

Their new "political consciousness" is really a form of racial consciousness.

Of all the racial, national, and cultural groups that have recently immigrated to the United States, Asians seem to enjoy the most positive stereotype. Everyone knows about Chinese immigrants who become computer wizards and Korean kids who make A's in calculus at the age of 12. Like most stereotypes, especially those promoted by the immigration lobby, it's not a very accurate one.

Asian youth gangs are no less a threat in cities where large numbers of Asians have settled than are gangs of other racial persuasions, and the last census showed that nearly a third of all Vietnamese immigrants to the United States were on welfare. Maybe by now they've all started their own software companies, but whatever they are, Asian immigrants in the United States are beginning to flex their political biceps.

NEW MOVEMENTS

The *New York Times* reports that Asian-Americans are starting to organize political movements to stop congressional efforts to limit immigration. This is new. In the past, Asians in the United States have tended to be rather passive politically, and the most aggressive pro-immigration lobbies have come from either Hispanic activist groups or such stalwarts of the far left as the National Lawyers Guild and Jack Kemp.

But Asians, according to the *Times*, are worried about congressional measures that aim to restrict legal immigration, so they've founded organizations for the purpose of smothering the legislation in its cradle and also for wheedling just a few more special privileges for themselves, their relatives and their buddies back home. Like most groups that demand special privileges, they want us to believe that these are their "rights."

CIVIL RIGHTS

Immigration, says the executive director of the National Asian Pacific American Legal Consortium, is the "cornerstone of what civil rights means to the community. We remember the simple issue of our race being thought not good enough to be allowed into the country, much less equal with other people." Other Asians like to invoke the internment of Japanese Americans by

Franklin Roosevelt as evidence of what could happen to them in the future once anti-immigration forces triumph.

But the internment of the Japanese, while a sorry chapter in the record of Roosevelt's contempt for liberty, was confined to Japanese during wartime and was never directed against all Asians. Nor is current immigration legislation. The measures the Asians are grousing about would cut back the current legal right of immigrants to import siblings and married children. The bills aim at curtailing what is called "chain immigration," which allows immigrants who may qualify to enter the country permanently to bring in relatives who don't qualify, and the bills apply to all immigrants, not just Asians.

RACIAL APPROACH

But Asians, it seems, do have an unusual number of kinfolks. More than 70 percent of the relatives of all immigrants awaiting entry under current law are Asians, according to the Immigration and Naturalization Service, and that's why Asians already here are so eager to pull the guts out of the proposed changes.

But the point about the new Asian "political consciousness," as the *Times* calls it, is not that Asians shouldn't come here or might become criminals or welfare cases. The point is that Asians are organizing as Asians, that their new "political consciousness" is

61

really a form of racial consciousness, based on what is good for "our race" and "our" numberless relatives back home rather than on what's good for the country they've just adopted.

Supporters of unrestricted immigration like Jack Kemp, Ted Kennedy and Linda Chavez invariably argue that new immigrants "assimilate," that they shake off the dusty garments of the cultures they come from and quickly garb themselves in bright new American costume. Indeed, to hear these xenophiles gabble on about the contributions of immigrants, they seem to prefer aliens to their own countrymen.

ASSIMILATION

But the new Asian activism in support of more immigration for themselves and their relatives and their race gives the lie to the "assimilationist" claims, as does the equally racial activism of the Hispanic immigration lobby. If Asian and Hispanic activists thought of themselves as Americans rather than as soldiers in a racial crusade, they'd be more concerned for the interests of their new country than for those of their race.

The meaning of the new racial and political consciousness, then, is not that immigrants assimilate but that, once enough immigrants of a particular race, nation or culture arrive, they start thinking in terms of their own group, support political action intended to benefit their own group and forget the interests of the country they've invited themselves to live in. What that leads to is not a melting pot of assimilation but the melted pots of Bosnia and Brazil. It might be wise for real Americans to think about what mass immigration really means for them and the country they and their ancestors created.

READING

9

ASIAN IMMIGRATION: THE COUNTERPOINT

Karen K. Narasaki

Karen K. Narasaki is the executive director of the National Asian Pacific American Legal Consortium. The following comments came before the House Judiciary Subcommittee on Immigration. The subcommittee was holding a hearing on immigration legislation.

■ POINTS TO CONSIDER

1. Describe the Chinese Exclusion Act and the Gentlemen's Agreement.

2. How were the Immigration Act of 1917 and the Quota Law of 1921 different?

3. What was unique about the Immigration and Naturalization Act of 1965?

4. Why was the Immigration Act of 1990 a failure for some people?

Excerpted from congressional testimony by Karen K. Narasaki before the House Judiciary Subcommittee on Immigration, June 29, 1995.

It is no secret that the history of this country's immigration laws has been fraught with racial bias.

The area of immigration policy is particularly important to the Consortium because of the large percentage of recent immigrants in the Asian Pacific American community and the long history of racially discriminatory treatment of Asians and Pacific Islanders by our country's immigration laws.

The Consortium and its affiliates, the Asian American Legal Defense and Education Fund in New York, the Asian Law Caucus in San Francisco and the Asian Pacific American Legal Center of Southern California, collectively have over half a century of experience in providing direct legal services, community education and advocacy on immigration law and immigrant rights issues.

We have not been able to obtain a copy of the actual legislation, so our comments will be limited to changes being proposed to the family immigration system, refugee numbers and to the enforcement of the employer sanctions provision of the Immigration Reform and Control Act. We note, however, that from what we have seen, we have serious concerns about due process issues in some of what appears to be proposed in other areas.

The Consortium believes that it is important that Congress not make immigration policy without first fully considering the historical context. For non-European immigrants, particularly those from Asia, repercussions of this country's discriminatory immigration laws are still being felt.

HISTORY OF DISCRIMINATORY IMMIGRATION LAWS

It is no secret that the history of this country's immigration laws has been fraught with racial bias. The Chinese Exclusion Act of 1882, which prohibited the immigration of Chinese laborers, epitomizes this country's particularly infamous record on immigration from Asia. In 1907, anti-Asian sentiment culminated in the Gentlemen's Agreement limiting Japanese immigration. Asian immigration was further restricted by the Immigration Act of 1917 which banned immigration from almost all countries in the Asia-Pacific region; the Quota Law of 1921 which limited the annual immigration of a given nationality to three percent of the number

64

of such persons residing in the U.S. as of 1910; and the National Origins Act of 1924 which banned immigration of persons who were ineligible for citizenship. A decade later, the Tydings-McDuffie Act of 1934 placed a quota of 50 Filipino immigrants per year.

It has been just one generation since the Chinese Exclusion Act and its progeny were repealed in 1943. Even after the repeal, discriminatory quotas were set using formulas giving special preference to immigration from Europe. Until 1965, for example, the German annual quota was almost 26,000 and the Irish almost 18,000 while the annual quota from China was 105, from Japan 185, the Philippines 100 and the Pacific Islands 100.

The intensity of the discrimination against immigrants from Asia is reflected in the fact that they were not allowed to become naturalized citizens for over 160 years. A 1790 law allowed only "free white persons" to become citizens. Even after the law was changed to include African Americans, similar legislation to include Asian Americans was rejected. The Supreme Court upheld the laws making Asian immigrants ineligible for citizenship. The last of these laws were not repealed until 1952.

Congress finally acknowledged the immorality of the racial bias imbedded in the immigration system with the passage of the Immigration and Naturalization Act of 1965, but did not redress the effect of earlier biases. In fact, the 20,000 per country limit, imposed without any connection to size of originating country or demand, resulted in extremely long waiting lists for Asian immigrants.

The Immigration Act of 1990 failed to address the tremendous backlogs that already existed for countries like Mexico, India, the Philippines, South Korea, China and Hong Kong. Instead, Congress exacerbated the problem by reducing the number of visas available for adult sons and daughters of U.S. citizens. At the time the backlog consisted primarily of children of Filipino veterans who are allowed to naturalize under the Act because of their service to this country in fighting in World War II. Despite this fact, Congress cut the quota in half and reduced other family categories causing the backlog to increase by close to 70%. Now, on the 50th anniversary of the end of World War II, this bill would deny these war heroes the comfort of their children in their waning years.

As a result, although Asians have constituted approximately 40% of this country's immigration for the past two decades, the community still constitutes less than 4% of the U.S. population, and well over 1.5 million Asian immigrants are still waiting in backlogs for entry visas to reunite with their families. Any additional restrictions or reduction in the overall numbers, particularly in the family preference categories, will have an inordinate impact on Asian Pacific American families.

PROPOSED CHANGES TO THE LEGAL IMMIGRATION SYSTEM

The Consortium, together with other Asian Pacific American community-based organizations such as the Organization of Chinese Americans, Japanese American Citizens League, Chinese for Affirmative Action, National Association of Korean Americans, Asian Pacific American Labor Alliance/AFL-CIO, and the National Asian Pacific American Bar Association, strongly opposes the proposed drastic reduction in legal immigration.

The bill under consideration by the Congress slashes family immigration to 330,000 from 512,000 estimated in 1994 and abolishes three of the four existing categories of family immigration. Adult children and brother and sister family preference categories would be eliminated. Only parents, minor children and spouses of U.S. citizens and legal permanent residents will be allowed to immigrate in the family categories. Special restrictions are placed on the ability of parents of U.S. citizens to immigrate. In addition, they have been reduced in priority and their numbers are capped at 50,000.

We question the necessity of any cuts in the current level of immigration. Annual taxes paid by immigrants to all levels of government more than offset the costs of services received, generating a net annual surplus of $25 billion to $30 billion. Moreover, immigrants have been a driving force behind urban revitalization. Asian, Latino, Caribbean and Russian Jewish immigrants revived dying neighborhoods in Brooklyn, New York. Asian and Russian Jewish immigrants have revitalized parts of Seattle, and Latinos revived a South Dallas neighborhood. Asian and Latino immigrants have been important to Atlanta, and Chinese immigrants brought back a long neglected industrial section of Los Angeles.

ORWELLIAN SYSTEM

Republicans in the House and Senate are moving quickly forward with Orwellian legislation that would create a national computerized registration system for all American workers. The new federal computer worker registry, which is intended to reduce illegal immigration, is the crucial first step toward the implementation of a national identification card system for all 120 million American workers. For the first time ever, employers would have to receive the government's permission to hire a new worker. Sen. Dianne Feinstein (D-CA) has even urged that the ID cards contain individuals' photographs, fingerprints, and even retina scans.

John J. Miller and Stephen Moore, "A National ID System", **Policy Analysis**, 7 Sept. 1995.

CONCLUSION

We need to focus on the national interest. But that national interest is not in conflict with the current system of immigration that we have today. The national interest is in working to revitalize our economy and maintaining our competitiveness in the global marketplace. The national interest is in our living up to our country's principles of fairness and equity and not reviving our shamefully discriminatory policies of the past. The national interest is in valuing and reuniting families, protecting due process and keeping government out of our private lives.

What has become lost in this debate is that immigration is about more than just numbers. Immigration is about people and about what kind of nation we want to be. One that stagnates because it wastes precious resources in playing the blame game or one that moves boldly toward our future by working on the real economic challenges we face today?

WHAT IS RACE BIAS?

This activity may be used as an individualized study guide for students in libraries and resource centers or as a discussion catalyst in small group and classroom discussions.

Many readers are unaware that written material usually expresses an opinion or bias. The skill to read with insight and understanding requires the ability to detect different kinds of bias. Political bias, race bias, sex bias, ethnocentric bias and religious bias are five basic kinds of opinions expressed in editorials and literature that attempt to persuade. This activity will focus on race bias defined in the glossary below.

Five Kinds of Editorial Opinion or Bias

- **Sex Bias** – the expression of dislike for and/or feeling of superiority over a person because of gender or sexual preference.

- **Race Bias** – the expression of dislike for and/or feeling of superiority over a racial group.

- **Ethnocentric Bias** – the expression of a belief that one's own group, race, religion, culture or nation is superior. Ethnocentric persons judge others by their own standards and values.

- **Political Bias** – the expression of opinions and attitudes about government-related issues on the local, state, national or international level.

- **Religious Bias** – the expression of a religious belief or attitude.

Guidelines

Read through the following statements and decide which ones represent race bias. Evaluate each statement by using the method indicated below.

- **Mark (R)** for any statements that reflect racial or ethnic bias.

- **Mark (F)** for any factual statements.

- **Mark (O)** for any statements of opinion that reflect other kinds of opinion or bias.

- **Mark (N)** for any statements that you are not sure about.

1. _____ Strict immigration legislation is a means for politicians to court votes.

2. _____ California's Proposition 187, a ballot initiative that would deny illegal immigrants social welfare benefits, is an attack on the Latino Community.

3. _____ The long-term, aggregate effect of immigration is positive culturally and economically, though it is seen as a societal drain in the short term.

4. _____ Legal and illegal immigrants place a burden on government social systems.

5. _____ The principle objective of legal immigration is family reunification.

6. _____ Pursuing more just social and economic foreign policies, particularly in Mexico, would eliminate much of the illegal immigration. In the meantime, it would be morally unacceptable for the United States to keep out the political and economic refugees crossing its borders.

7. _____ Illegal immigrants are necessary to fill the large number of poorly paid, unskilled positions that native-born Americans cannot or will not fill.

8. _____ Welfare payment to immigrants – legal or illegal – of working age is extremely low, substantially lower than payment to natives.

9._____ Welfare benefits should be denied to legal, as well as illegal immigrants in order to encourage the immigration of productive citizens.

10._____ Large numbers of poorly paid, unskilled refugees and immigrants threaten the wages of the nation as a whole.

11._____ Latino immigration has hurt traditional American culture.

12._____ Welfare reformers are overconcerned with the immigration issue.

13._____ It is a national responsibility to supply those within our borders with assistance if needed.

14._____ Serious Congressional measures which would deny legal immigration are only serving to fuel an unfounded anti-immigrant hysteria.

15._____ There are ethnocentric and racist undertones in the immigration debate.

16._____ Beyond the various moral and social consequences, our nation cannot ignore the serious economic strains of immigration.

17._____ It is the federal government's responsibility to financially assist states such as California with severe illegal immigration problems.

18._____ Most people do not care to recognize how dependent the U.S. economy is upon the source of cheap labor gained through illegal immigration.

Other Activities

1. Locate three examples of **racial** or **ethnic bias** in the readings from Chapter Two.

2. Make up one-sentence statements that would be an example of each of the following: **sex bias, race bias, ethnocentric bias, and religious bias.**

CHAPTER 3

THE PUBLIC COST OF IMMIGRATION

port, sponsors attest to their ability and willingness to provide financial assistance to the immigrant. However, several courts have ruled that these affidavits of support are not legally binding.

Immigrants and Citizens

Overall, immigrants as a group are more likely than citizens to be receiving SSI or AFDC benefits. Based on Consumer Price Statistics (CPS) data, immigrants receiving SSI or AFDC represented about 6 percent of all immigrants in 1993; in contrast, about 3.4 percent of citizens received such assistance. However, the total number of immigrants receiving SSI or AFDC is much lower than the number of citizens because legal immigrants represent only about 6 percent of the U.S. population. Based on 1993 administrative data, an estimated 18.6 million citizens received SSI or AFDC, compared with an estimated 1.4 million legal immigrants.

Much of the difference in recipiency rates between immigrants and citizens can be explained by differences in their demographic characteristics and household composition. Immigrants are much more likely than citizens to be poor. In 1993, about 29 percent of immigrant households reported incomes below the poverty line, compared with 14 percent of citizen households. Researchers have noted that immigrant households have larger numbers of small children and elderly or disabled persons and contain more members with relatively little schooling and low skill levels. These are all characteristics that increase the likelihood of welfare recipiency. Public policy has also played a role in immigrants' receipt of public assistance. Refugees and asylees are categories of immigrants who are much more likely to be on welfare than citizens or other immigrants. By virtue of their refugee or asylee status alone, they qualify immediately for assistance programs that may be restricted to other immigrants.

Almost 83 percent of all immigrants receiving SSI or AFDC in 1993 resided in four states: California, New York, Florida, and Texas. This is not surprising given that over 68 percent of all immigrants resided in these states. Over one-half of the immigrants receiving these benefits lived in California.

B. ILLEGAL IMMIGRANTS AND PUBLIC ASSISTANCE

In recent years, growing public concern about illegal aliens in the United States has focused on their use of public benefits and

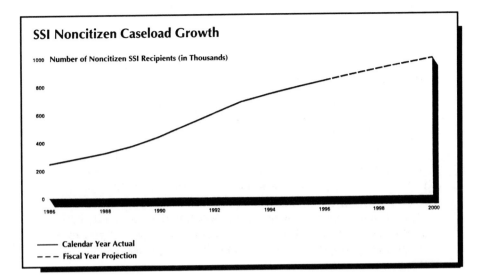

SSI Noncitizen Caseload Growth

1000 **Number of Noncitizen SSI Recipients (in Thousands)**

800

600

400

200

0

1986   1988   1990   1992   1994   1996   1998   2000

——— **Calendar Year Actual**
– – – **Fiscal Year Projection**

Source: Social Security Administration

their overall costs to society. Some 3-1/2 to 4 million illegal aliens resided in the United States in 1994, according to government estimates. States' concerns about the strain on their budgets from providing public benefits and services to illegal aliens have prompted six states to file suit against the federal government for reimbursement of some of these costs. In one state, California, voters recently passed a measure that would deny state-funded public benefits to illegal aliens, including education, non-emergency health services, and other social services.

Because illegal aliens not only receive public benefits but also pay taxes, we examined estimates of the public net cost of illegal aliens: the government costs they generate, minus the revenues they contribute to government.

Studies

In developing this information, we identified 13 studies of the net costs of illegal aliens issued between 1984 and 1994; only three of these studies estimated the national net cost, and we examined them in detail. They are (1) Donald Huddle's initial study of 1992 net costs, "The Costs of Immigration;" (2) the Urban Institute's critique of that study, "How Much Do Immigrants Really Cost? A Reappraisal of Huddle's 'The Cost of Immigrants';" and (3) Huddle's updated study, "The Net National Costs of Immigration in 1993." In addition, we consulted various experts in the field of immigration about issues that arose in assessing estimates of the fiscal impact of illegal aliens.

All three national studies concluded that illegal aliens in the United States generate more in costs than revenues to federal, state, and local governments combined. However, their estimates of the national net cost varied considerably, ranging from $2 billion to $19 billion.

Donald Huddle estimated that the national net cost of illegal aliens to federal, state, and local governments was $11.9 billion in 1992. This estimate was followed by an Urban Institute review of Huddle's work, which adjusted some of Huddle's cost and revenue estimates and estimated a much lower net cost for 1992 – $1.9 billion. Responding to the Urban Institute's criticisms, Huddle subsequently produced an updated estimate for 1993 that was higher than his initial estimate – $19.3 billion.

The States

Illegal immigration is an important issue, especially in California, New York, Texas, Florida, Illinois, Arizona, and New Jersey – the states estimated to account for over three-fourths of the illegal alien population. Illegal aliens are a concern not only because they are breaking immigration laws but for various other reasons. For example, state and local governments are especially concerned about the effect on their budgets of providing benefits and services to illegal aliens. In addition, there are concerns about whether the presence of illegal alien workers has negative effects on the employment of U.S. workers.

Illegal aliens are not eligible for most federal benefit programs, including Supplemental Security Income (SSI), Aid to Families With Dependent Children (AFDC), food stamps, unemployment compensation, financial assistance for higher education, and the Job Training Partnership Act (JTPA). However, they may participate in certain benefit programs that do not require legal immigration status as a condition of eligibility, such as Head Start, the Special Supplemental Food Program for Women, Infants, and Children (WIC), and the school lunch program. In addition, they are eligible for emergency medical services, including childbirth services, under Medicaid if they meet the program's conditions of eligibility. Illegal aliens may apply for AFDC and food stamps on behalf of their U.S. citizen children. Although it is the child and not the parent in such cases who qualifies for the programs, benefits help support the child's family.

NON-CITIZENS

Non-citizens, who include legal immigrants and refugees, accounted for nearly 25 percent of SSI's caseload growth from 1986 through 1993. In December 1995, almost 800,000 non-citizens were receiving SSI benefits, accounting for about 12 percent of all SSI recipients. In 1995, federal and state SSI benefits to non-citizens totaled nearly $4 billion.

In addition to federal SSI benefits, states may provide supplemental benefits. In December 1995, nearly 40 percent of SSI recipients received an average of about $105 per month in state supplemental benefits at a total cost to the states of about $3.2 billion a year. Most SSI recipients are generally eligible for Medicaid and food stamps, which can cost the government more than SSI benefits themselves.

Jane L. Ross, "Supplemental Security Income," General Accounting Office report, May 23, 1996.

Illegal aliens may not work in the United States or legally obtain Social Security numbers for work purposes. However, many illegal aliens do work and have Social Security taxes withheld from their wages based on falsely obtained numbers. Illegal aliens are not explicitly barred from receiving Social Security benefits; nonetheless, some illegal aliens may not be able to collect benefits because an individual generally must have obtained a valid Social Security number to receive credit for work performed.

Illegal aliens generate revenues as well as costs; these revenues offset some of the costs that governments incur. Research studies indicate that many illegal aliens pay taxes, including federal and state income taxes; Social Security tax; and sales, gasoline, and property taxes. However, researchers disagree on the amount of revenues illegal aliens generate and the extent to which these revenues offset government costs for benefits and services.

READING

11

WELFARE IS A RETIREMENT PLAN FOR FOREIGNERS

Robert Rector

Robert Rector is a senior policy analyst for the Heritage Foundation in Washington, D.C. The Heritage Foundation is a leading source of policy ideas for conservative members of Congress.

■ POINTS TO CONSIDER

1. Why is the U.S. becoming a retirement home for the elderly of foreign countries?

2. How does the author describe the cost of SSI and Medicaid benefits for elderly non-citizen recipients?

3. What immigrants should sponsors be responsible for supporting financially?

4. Summarize the author's recommendations for changing immigration policy.

Excerpted from congressional testimony by Robert T. Rector before the Senate Judiciary Subcommittee on Immigration, February 6, 1996.

Immigration should be open to a limited number of individuals who wish to come to the United States to work and be self-sufficient.

The United States welfare system is rapidly becoming a deluxe retirement home for the elderly of other countries. This is because many individuals are now immigrating to the United States in order to obtain generous welfare that far exceeds programs available in their country of origin. Non-citizens today are among the fastest growing groups of welfare dependents.

In 1994, there were nearly 738,000 lawful non-citizen residents receiving aid from the Supplemental Security Insurance (SSI) program. This was up from 127,900 in 1982 – a 580 percent increase in just 12 years. The overwhelming majority of non-citizen SSI recipients are elderly. Most apply for welfare within five years of arriving in the United States.

The data show that welfare is becoming a way of life for elderly immigrants. An analysis of elderly immigrants in California by Professor Norman Matloff of the University of California at Davis shows that 45 percent received cash welfare in 1990. Among Russian immigrants, the figure is 66 percent; among Chinese, 55 percent. Worse, the trend is accelerating. Recent immigrants are far more likely to become welfare dependents than those who arrived in the United States in earlier decades.

CURRENT TRENDS

If current trends continue, the U.S. will have more than three million non-citizens on SSI within ten years. Without reform, the total cost of SSI and Medicaid benefits for elderly non-citizen immigrants will amount to over $328 billion over the next ten years. Annual SSI and Medicaid benefits for these individuals will reach over $67 billion per year in 2004.

Even with the implausible assumption that the current rapid increase of non-citizen recipients will halt and the number of elderly immigrants receiving benefits will remain at current levels, U.S. taxpayers would still pay over $127 billion over the next ten years for SSI and Medicaid benefits for resident aliens.

Congressional testimony by Dr. Matloff demonstrates that immigrants have a high degree of awareness of welfare policies and procedures. Besides word of mouth among immigrants, sources in foreign countries as well as in the United States give advice on how to obtain welfare benefits. For example, Zai Meiguo Sheng Huo Xu Zhi ("What You Need to Know About Life in America"), a publication sold in Taiwan and Hong Kong, and in Chinese bookstores in the U.S., includes a 36-page guide to SSI and other welfare benefits. The largest-circulation Chinese-language newspaper in the U.S., *Shijie Ribao (World Journal)*, runs a regular "Dear Abby"-style advice column on SSI and other immigration-related matters.

WELFARE

Prudent restrictions on providing welfare to recent immigrants long has been part of the American tradition. Becoming a charge was grounds for deportation in the Massachusetts Bay colony even before the American Revolution. America's first immigration law, passed by Congress in 1882, prohibited the entry of paupers and persons who were likely to become public charges. Similar restrictions have appeared in subsequent immigration law. Today, the Immigration and Nationality Act declares unequivocally: "Any alien who, within five years after the date of entry, has become a public charge from causes not affirmatively shown to have arisen since entry is deportable." The problem is that this provision of the law is ignored.

The presence of large numbers of elderly immigrants on welfare is a violation of the spirit, and arguably the letter, of U.S. immigration law. The relatives who sponsored the entry of these individuals into the U.S. implicitly promised that the new immigrants would not become a burden to the U.S. taxpayer. But many, if not most, sponsors are enrolling their elderly immigrant relatives on welfare soon after the end of the three-year waiting period. Once on SSI, there is every indication that these immigrants will remain on welfare indefinitely.

Although many of the elderly non-citizens on SSI come from politically oppressive nations such as Cuba or the former Soviet Union, the majority do not. The single greatest number of aliens on SSI come from Mexico. Other nations, such as the Dominican Republic, India, South Korea, and the Philippines, also contribute large numbers of recipients.

Moreover, while Americans greatly sympathize with those individuals who have suffered from political oppression and econom-

Cartoon by Steve Kelly. Reprinted with permission of **Coply News Service**.

ic failure inherent to communist regimes, U.S. welfare programs are not appropriate vehicles to redress that suffering, nor should they serve as a retirement program for these individuals. Just as the United States military cannot serve as a global policeman, U.S. welfare programs cannot serve as a global retirement system.

SPONSORS

Most non-citizens on SSI lawfully admitted to the U.S. have relatives capable of supporting them. To have brought a relative to the U.S. in the first place, the sponsor must have demonstrated a capacity to support that relative. And most sponsors do, in fact, support their immigrant relatives for at least three years after their arrival. If SSI benefits for non-citizens were terminated, in most cases the family support which sustained the immigrant immediately after arrival in the U.S. simply would be resumed.

Just as Americans expect an absent parent to pay child support for his children, so they also must expect individuals who voluntarily bring elderly and near-elderly relatives to the U.S. to support those relatives fully. This obligation to support should be permanent and should not be limited to three or five years as under the current law. Under no circumstances should the cost of supporting elderly and near-elderly immigrants to the United States be passed to the general taxpayer.

POLICY RECOMMENDATIONS

The U.S. has a huge welfare system with over 80 major programs. In 1993, federal and state spending on means-tested programs providing cash, food, housing, medical care, training, and social services to low income persons amounted to $324 billion or 5 percent of GDP.

An advanced welfare state has to be very careful in designing its immigration policy. A welfare state will place great strains on its taxpayers if it encourages the immigration of large numbers of:

1) elderly and near-elderly persons; or

2) low-skilled persons.

Dramatic change in both the current welfare system and in immigration policy is required. Eligibility for Supplemental Security Income and Medicaid should be restricted to U.S. citizens. However, such a restriction provides a mammoth loophole since welfare eligibility to elderly immigrants cannot be limited after they become citizens. Thus limiting the growth of the SSI and Medicaid caseloads requires not only limiting benefits to noncitizens, but also to reducing the number of elderly immigrants who enter the country in the future.

In the future, elderly and near-elderly foreigners should be permitted to enter the U.S. only as guests of American relatives who sponsor them. Such elderly "guests" would not have the option of becoming citizens and thereby becoming a future burden on the U.S. taxpayer; they should be supported permanently by the relative who sponsored their entry.

Simply requiring that sponsors provide medical insurance to immigrating elderly relatives is not sufficient. First of all, there is no practical way to assure that the insurance will really be provided five or ten years after the immigrant's entry. Second, once the immigrant becomes a citizen, there is no lawful way to keep him or her off SSI, Medicaid or any other welfare program. And once the elderly immigrant has become a citizen, there is no lawful means to require the sponsor to provide health insurance or defer

NO LEGAL RIGHT

It is unfair to force citizens of any country or state to provide public benefits to those who have no legal right to be there. The mass of illegal aliens in California, Texas, and Florida now numbers in the millions; it dramatizes the need not for bigger social budgets but for effective border control. Former Supreme Court Justice William Brennan and other imaginative judges have claimed that the Fourteenth Amendment's equal protections apply to illegal residents. This is an exercise in hallucination. The Fourteenth Amendment explicitly protects "citizens of the United States," and in particular their "property."

Paul Gottfried, "Citizens, Immigrants and Aliens," **The American Enterprise,** March-April, 1995.

welfare costs. Thus, the only real mechanism for reducing the growth in the number of elderly immigrants on welfare is to reduce the number of such immigrants who enter the U.S. with the option of eventually becoming citizens.

U.S. immigration policy should also dramatically reduce the number of low-skilled, poorly-educated immigrants and should increase the relative share of highly-skilled immigrants. This can be accomplished by dramatically reducing the number of relatives entering by way of family preference under current law.

Overall, immigration should be open to a limited number of individuals who wish to come to the United States to work and be self-sufficient and who clearly have the capacity to support themselves. America should open its doors to those who have skills and seek opportunity. But immigration should not become an avenue to welfare dependence.

READING

12

IMMIGRANTS DO NOT COME FOR PUBLIC BENEFITS

Victor DoCouto

Victor DoCouto is executive director of the Massachusetts Alliance of Portuguese Speakers (MAPS). MAPS is dedicated to providing cultur- ally and linguistically competent services in Greater Boston to the Portuguese-speaking community which includes individuals from Portugal (Azores, Madeira and the continent), Brazil, Cape Verde, Angola, Guinea Bissau, Macau, Mozambique, Sao Tome and Timor.

■ POINTS TO CONSIDER

1. How have immigrants contributed to the American economy?

2. Why should immigrants retain their eligibility for SSI and other public benefits?

3. Under what circumstances should sponsors be held responsible for the costs of immigrants?

4. Why would it be wrong to deny public assistance to immigrants?

Excerpted from congressional testimony before the Senate Judiciary Subcommittee on Immigration, February 6, 1996.

In aggregate, immigrants pay $25 billion more in taxes annually than they receive in benefits.

Immigrants come to the U.S. primarily to reunite with family members already in the country and to improve their economic lot in life. They, as most people, wish to live near family members and will work hard to retain family connections and join their loved ones in the U.S.

IMMIGRANTS' WORK

In Massachusetts, many industries were built on the backs of immigrant labor, including labor-intensive work in the fishing industry, at textile mills, the shoe and furniture industries, to name a few. Over the years, these industries have either become highly automated so that many workers' jobs were phased out or the industry disappeared altogether, or companies have moved their manufacturing base to areas with less expensive labor costs.

Immigrants today staff service industries such as cleaning services, food chains, hospitals and nursing homes. Even if these jobs are well below an individual's work capacity, immigrants are willing to work these physically demanding, generally low pay/no benefit jobs. Although these jobs are often ones that native Americans consider beneath them, immigrants are willing to do them to have the opportunity for a better economic life here and to achieve their most important goal, family reunification.

WHY SHOULD IMMIGRANTS RETAIN THEIR ELIGIBILITY FOR SSI?

There currently is a heated debate as to whether immigrants are a benefit or a burden to the U.S. The reality is that most immigrants work, pay taxes, register for military service, and support programs which benefit U.S. citizens. According to the Urban Institute, in aggregate, immigrants pay $25 billion more in taxes annually than they receive in benefits.

In the context of the current debate, the question also comes up whether immigrants should retain their eligibility for public benefits, including SSI, under any circumstances. Some proposals are to bar immigrants from SSI altogether. Others exempt certain discrete groups of immigrants from the SSI ban while others, though not banning immigrants outright, exclude them through the deeming process.

Before addressing the specific SSI question for immigrants, I would like to stress that immigrants do not come to the U.S. with the goal of obtaining or living on government benefits. In fact, that is the furthest thing from an immigrant's mind. As I have mentioned, the primary reasons immigrants come to the U.S. are to improve their economic lot, to join family members and to make life anew with the people they care most about. It is my experience that immigrants do anything they can to avoid going to the welfare or Social Security offices. Obtaining the pension they earned through work at retirement is one thing, but getting help along the way is generally distasteful to immigrants. My experience, and statistics bear me out on this, is that the great majority of immigrants are industrious, hard-working, taxpaying, law abiding, financial contributors to our society. If anything, we want to become a member of society, honoring our culture and history, but doing our work and living our life with our families. Immigrants do not want to do anything to jeopardize their ability to live and work in this country. Receiving welfare is considered a disgrace, and not something that anyone does without painful consideration.

CIRCUMSTANCES

Notwithstanding these concerns, immigrants, as all other people, sometimes are faced with unfortunate circumstances and need help. Illness, disability, layoff, and other personal and family emergencies are as unpredictable for immigrants as they are for citizens. Immigrants, just as citizens, might need government-funded medical services due to illness or injury. Because immigrants often work in jobs without benefits, they are sometimes forced to seek this help from the government. And sometimes people may not be able to return to work at all, therefore needing cash assistance as well. In these times of crises, immigrants who "play by the rules" should be able to access safety net programs to which their tax dollars contribute.

Retired immigrant workers also need SSI. Often, employment options for immigrants are limited to unskilled, low-wage, no-benefit jobs. Indeed, they may have worked their whole life in such a position. I have met immigrants who have worked forty or more hours a week for decades but, because of their low pay, retire with a Social Security benefit of only $100 to $200 per month. These tireless workers, who have paid into the system for years,

86

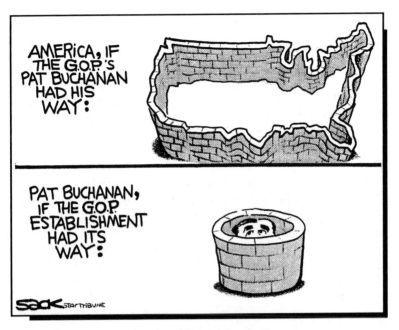

AMERICA, IF THE G.O.P.'S PAT BUCHANAN HAD HIS WAY:

PAT BUCHANAN, IF THE G.O.P. ESTABLISHMENT HAD ITS WAY:

Sack STAR TRIBUNE

Reprinted with permission from **Star Tribune**, Minneapolis.

should not be barred from the SSI program simply because they were not born a native American.

Other immigrants who might also need assistance through SSI include widows. Many immigrant women did what was expected of them and managed their homes for husbands and families. If their husbands precede them in death, they often need SSI to meet their basic needs.

In addition, sons and daughters of immigrant parents, who are themselves U.S. citizens, may not be economically able to take care of their parents in any degree greater than sons and daughters of native born citizens. Our economy today requires many families to work two and three jobs to take care of their own survival. Although sons and daughters may be able to contribute some to the cost of care of their retired or elderly parents, many immigrant families – just as middle-class Americans – could not meet the financial burdens of aging parents' medical or long-term care needs. Such elders should not be barred from SSI, simply because they are not native-born U.S. citizens.

ROLES/RESPONSIBILITIES OF SPONSORS

The question is also raised as to why sponsors should not be held responsible for the costs of immigrants living in the U.S. The answer is that sponsors do care for the immigrants they bring to this country. Under current law, sponsors' income is counted as available to immigrants in times of crisis for three to five years for AFDC, food stamps, and SSI programs. In addition, sponsors – especially blood relatives – often assist family members in meeting both day-to-day and emergency needs.

Various proposals in Congress propose extending the deeming requirements to many programs well beyond traditional welfare programs and well beyond the current time limits. Although many sponsors contribute to the specific immigrants whom they sponsor, many people who are sponsors are workers themselves who contribute to the support of programs through their taxes. Although sponsors could be held to greater accountability within the current deeming structure, extending sponsors' obligations through deeming for the lifetime or until citizenship of the sponsored immigrant is an unfair burden on sponsors.

The deeming requirements would be particularly harsh on some immigrants. For example, low-wage workers might never earn enough in "qualifying work quarters" to qualify for Social Security; homemakers – who worked at home without pay – would never escape the deemed income of their sponsors, and disabled people who, because of an illness or accident before working the requisite number of quarters, would never be free of the deeming requirement.

Some proposals even extend deeming beyond citizenship. Under this idea, even immigrants who become citizens would not be eligible for assistance in a time of crisis or at retirement unless they worked and paid income tax for 40 quarters. This would be a fundamental change in U.S. policy and, for the first time in history, would create two classes of citizens. This unprecedented distinction between American citizens born on U.S. soil and those who naturalize would be unacceptable.

MASSACHUSETTS STATISTICS OF PEOPLE ON SSI

In Massachusetts, these proposals would have an incredibly harsh impact. According to the Department of Public Welfare's December, 1993 "Facts and Figures Report" of SSI caseload num-

FOREIGN-BORN INCOME

The 1990 Census reports that the per capita income of foreign-born actually exceeded that of the native-born Americans. Much evidence suggest that children of immigrants are among the most productive members of American society.

Just as the free flow of goods, services, capital and ideas enhances the wealth of nations, so the free movement of people serves to better utilize the talents of our labor force, enhancing worldwide labor productivity and expanding incomes. Immigration increases our human capital and our rate of physical capital formation, adding vitality to our economy.

Richard Vedder, "Immigrants Benefit U.S. Society," **The Milwaukee Journal**, April 16, 1995.

bers, Massachusetts had a total number of 144,175 SSI recipients. Social Security Administration data from December, 1993, in which the actual number of citizens and non-citizens are tracked showed that 14% of the caseload were non-citizens. Of these, 14,710 people were Legal Permanent Residents and 5,530 were Permanently Residing Under Color of Law.

ABILITY OF AGENCIES LIKE MAPS TO MEET THE SERVICE NEEDS OF PEOPLE DENIED SSI

If the Senate votes to exclude legally present immigrants from SSI as well as from other basic support and health care programs, whether it be through a categorical ban or through some extension of the deeming process, states and localities will be faced with having to pick up the cost of income support and medical care for very vulnerable people. That is, by definition, the current population on SSI. This would require states, cities and town to absorb substantial costs for which they have not currently budgeted. Failing an extension of benefits to the SSI population, we can only expect a rise in the number of homeless, destitute and dying people, many of them elderly.

With all due respect, it is unrealistic to imagine that charitable organizations and agencies like MAPS will be able to replace lost

89

government supports and provide basic income and health care to legally present immigrants. Although some increase in volunteerism and charitable giving might be possible, it is impossible for public agencies and private charities to assume the enormous responsibility of providing basic income support to the poor, elderly disabled.

CONCLUSION

I hope that in considering immigrants for public benefits, particularly SSI, you will reconsider the enormous contributions which immigrants have made and continue to make through their work, their taxes, culture and family life to the U.S. economy and society. Immigrants are a rich resource for this nation. It is essential that their safety net through the SSI program be maintained.

READING

13

A NEGATIVE IMPACT ON WORKERS

Norman Matloff

Dr. Norman Matloff is a professor of computer science at the University of California at Davis, where he formerly was a professor of statistics. He writes frequently about minority and immigration issues.

Professor Matloff was a former Chair of the Affirmative Action Committee at UC Davis, and has long been active in work supporting minorities, particularly African-Americans and Latino-Americans. He has been close to immigrant communities all his life. He spent part of his formative years in predominantly Latino East Los Angeles, and his father was an immigrant from Lithuania.

■ **POINTS TO CONSIDER**

1. Why does the current rate of immigration have some negative impacts on society?

2. Briefly summarize these negative impacts.

3. How are some African-American and Asian-American workers affected by immigration?

4. What do minority populations say about current rates of immigration?

5. According to the author, what is the best way to measure the effects of immigration on minorities?

Excerpted from congressional testimony by Norman Matloff before the House Judiciary Subcommittee on Immigration and Claims, April 5, 1995.

As Cornell University economist Vernon Briggs has said, the effort "to raise disadvantaged urban black Americans out of poverty was undermined from the beginning by the flood of cheap foreign labor."

We are indeed a nation of immigrants. In fact, though a stereotypical American would have British ancestors who came to this continent during the 1700s if not earlier, the fact is that rather few of us fit that description.

The adventurous spirits of those who came to this country in earlier times contributed greatly to America's success. Immigration continues to add vitality to our society today. Yet conditions have changed significantly from those earlier times, and the current high rate of immigration does have its down sides. One very important class of down sides is the adverse impact immigration has on minorities. In particular:

- Immigration adversely impacts native-born African-Americans.

- Immigration adversely impacts both native-born and earlier-arriving immigrant Asian-Americans and Latino-Americans.

- These adverse impacts are due to both legal and illegal immigration.

- Some of these adverse impacts are economic in nature, in the form of increased job competition, lowered wages and reduced opportunities for entrepreneurs.

- Other adverse impacts are non-economic, such as reductions in quality of education and housing, and increased exposure to disease.

- Immigration is resulting in diminished attention being paid to the problems of native-born minorities. In some ways, this problem is even more serious than those cited above.

- Poll after poll in recent years has shown that minorities recognize these adverse impacts, and wish for relief, in the form of reduced levels of both legal and illegal immigration.

ECONOMIC ASPECTS

On a general societal level, the economic impacts of immigration are exceedingly complex, and virtually impossible to analyze.

Furthermore, though some really top-flight economists specialize in immigration issues, macro-level, economic analyses have their limitations.

As a professional statistician, I wish to emphasize that it is vital to keep in mind that statistical methodology is at best something to be resorted to when one merely has numbers in lieu of insight. Number-crunching alone cannot replace qualitative insights which come from intimate knowledge of immigrant communities. Immigration economists who spend their time in front of computer terminals instead of in immigrant communities are working blindly, merely speculating as to the meanings of their numbers. Indeed, often they do not even know which numbers are the most relevant to analyze.

In short, it is the author's view that direct observation, especially by those who understand minority communities, provides the most reliable gauge of immigration's economic impacts, including impacts on minorities. Here are some examples of adverse economic impacts on minorities:

- When asked why most Latino-Americans wish to see reduced immigration, Antonia Hernandez, president of the Mexican American Legal Defense and Educational Fund (MALDEF), explained that "migration, legal and undocumented, does have an impact on our economy...particularly in competition within the Latino community...There is an issue of wage depression, as in the garment industry, which is predominantly immigrant, of keeping wages down because of the flow of traffic of people."

- Presumably motivated by similar concerns of job competition, United Farm Workers co-founder Dolores Huerta testified to a California Assembly committee that "with 1.5 million legalized immigrants living in California, and only approximately 250,000 agricultural jobs in the state, there is no need for additional farm workers."

- Immigrants are entering the U.S. faster than minority communities can absorb them. Numerous case studies in New York's Chinese-American community by sociologist Hsiang-Shui Chen show how the influx of Chinese newcomers – both legal and illegal – reduces employment opportunity for native and earlier-immigrant Chinese, as well as resulting in reduced market shares for established Chinese entrepreneurs.

Louisiana State University sociologist Min Zhou makes similar comments, discussing the low wages in New York's Chinatown, caused by "the large pool of surplus immigrant labor." The same themes show up in the study by Peter Kwong of Hunter College. Here is a very telling excerpt, on the hardships faced by native-born and earlier-arriving immigrant entrepreneurs, caused by the arrivals of large numbers of later immigrants:

> In the 1980s, business in Chinatown reached the point of saturation: too many new businesses, and exhorbitant rents. Suicidal competition developed throughout the community.

Similar dynamics appear to be at work among Korean immigrants in New York. An article in *New York* magazine quotes Sung Soo Kim, president of the Korean-American Small Business Service Center: "We're in the middle of a tragedy. Last year, we had 700 stores open but 900 close. Growth has completely stopped."

- A 1988 study of the Los Angeles hotel industry by the General Accounting Office found that jobs formerly held by African-Americans were now performed mainly by immigrants. Again, this study was not based on some econometric model. On the contrary, it was a direct report of the hotel owners' actions to break up the largely-black unions, and replacement by immigrant workers. Studies have shown a similar displacement of blacks in the restaurant industry, at airports, and so on.

- Jack Miles of the *Los Angeles Times* has found that even black social workers are being displaced by Latinos. The blacks hope to keep their jobs by learning Spanish, but this may or may not succeed. Ezola Foster, a black Los Angeles school teacher, describes a similar situation for teachers.

- The competition for jobs was illustrated in a rather dramatic manner in an article, "Immigrants Split Over Job Scarcity: Legal Residents in Marin Tell INS [Immigration and Naturalization Service] About Illegals," in the May 17, 1994 edition of the *San Francisco Chronicle*. The lead sentence in the article reports, "A shortage of jobs is provoking cutthroat rivalry among immigrant day laborers in San Rafael's Canal Area, where legal immigrants are getting ahead by turning in their undocumented peers to the INS, authorities say."

Persons Naturalized by Year: FYs 1910-1995

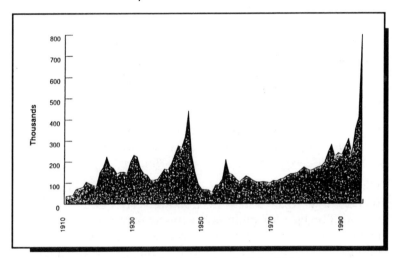

Source: Immigration and Naturalization Service, Statistics Division

• The adverse economic impact on minorities is not restricted to the low end of the wage scale. Asian-Americans, who comprise more than 50% of new graduates of computer science curricula in California universities, are often shunted aside by Silicon Valley employers in favor of foreign nationals. Computer industry employers continue to hire the foreign nationals and sponsor them for immigration or work visas, in spite of a labor surplus which has existed since the late 1980s. Often the employers' motivation is a desire for cheap, compliant labor. One General Dynamics subcontractor has even referred to the foreign employees' status as being "indentured."

Even Stanford Law Professor Bill Ong Hing, a nationally prominent immigrant-rights advocate, has expressed concern over the impact of hiring of foreign professionals on our nation's minorities.

JOBS AND IMMIGRATION

In other words, the frequently-heard adage, "Immigrants take jobs which Americans don't want," simply does not jibe with reality. In those hotel jobs described above, for instance, the African-Americans had wanted those jobs and indeed had been working in them. As Cornell University economist Vernon Briggs has said,

95

the effort "to raise disadvantaged urban black Americans out of poverty was undermined from the beginning by the flood of cheap foreign labor."

And it is said that many analysts who defend the current high immigration levels concede but dismiss the adverse economic impacts of later-arriving immigrants on earlier-arriving immigrants. Those earlier-arriving immigrants are now Americans, after all, and any concerns we have that immigration reduces economic opportunities for Americans must include these new Americans. I find it odd that many who defend immigration do not defend immigrants.

On the other hand, cheap wages do not tell the whole story. Another major factor is networked hiring. News of job openings are spread by tight social networks among immigrants, alleviating the employer of the need to advertise. As a result, says Richard Rothstein, a columnist for the Spanish-language *La Opinion*, "In the garment districts of Los Angeles, New York, or Miami, entire plants are staffed by immigrants from the same village in Mexico, El Salvador or China." Significantly, Rothstein adds that "once such powerful networks are established, policy is impotent to break them."

And again, networked hiring is not limited to the low end of the wage scale. Chinese immigrant engineers in the Silicon Valley are also frequently hired via Chinese social networks. It is common to find that most or all of a division in a company consists of immigrants from Taiwan. Since hiring is often done via word of mouth, those who are not from Taiwan may not even be aware of job openings.

Some employers hire immigrants because they are perceived to be reliable. Peter Skerry notes that Latino workers in Los Angeles tend to use carpools to get to work, whereas a black worker might not show up for work if his car breaks down. Indeed, questions might be raised along the lines of "Why blame the immigrants? Why can't blacks form networks, use carpools, etc.?" The answer is that although it is true that many poor blacks lack these work skills, the continuing influx of large numbers of immigrants is working to insure that poor blacks never will develop these skills. The availability of immigrant labor is certainly giving employers no incentives to develop skills among poor blacks.

JOB CREATION BY IMMIGRANTS

Immigrant advocates claim that immigrants (legal and illegal), through entrepreneurship and consumerism, are creating many jobs for native-borns. This is a serious oversimplification. Immigrant entrepreneurs tend to operate within immigrant communities, and thus they tend to hire other immigrants, not native-borns. Similarly, immigrant consumers tend to patronize immigrant-owned businesses.

USE OF WELFARE SERVICES

Immigrant advocates state that "immigrants come here for jobs, not welfare. Also, they pay more in taxes than they receive in services." This is misleading in multiple senses. Undocumented people come to the U.S. mainly for economic reasons. This of course includes jobs, but it also includes welfare. As mentioned earlier, some immigrant advocates and ethnic community leaders now admit that welfare is a magnet which attracts many elderly legal immigrants to the U.S. It would be reasonable to assume from this that a number of illegal immigrants also find welfare attractive. In any case, as seen above, incomes of illegal families are so low that they are forced to turn to welfare to make ends meet, even if that was not their original intent.

READING

14

A POSITIVE IMPACT ON THE WORKFORCE

Julian Simon

*Julian L. Simon is a professor of business administration at the University of Maryland and an adjunct scholar of the Cato Institute and the Heritage Foundation. He is the author of many books, includ-*ing The Economics of Population Growth, The Ultimate Resource, *and* The Economics of Immigration, *and editor of* The State of Humanity *from Basil Blackwell.*

■ POINTS TO CONSIDER

1. Summarize the effect that immigrants have on employment and on wages.

2. What is the Vedder-Gallaway-Moore study?

3. Describe the Fix-Passel review of U.S. unemployment and earnings.

4. How has immigration affected less skilled workers?

5. Explain the effect of immigration on minority populations.

Julian Simon, "Immigration: The Demographic and Economic Facts," Cato Institute and the National Immigration Forum, 1995. Excerpts reprinted by permission.

"There is no evidence...that illegal immigration had a significant adverse effect on the earnings opportunities of any native group, including blacks."

Displacement of citizens from employment by immigrants has always been one of the major fears about immigration. Englishman John Toland wrote in 1714, "The vulgar, I confess, are seldom pleas'd in a country with the coming in of Foreners...from their grudging at more persons sharing the same trades or business with them." But Toland also explained why this fear need not be realized. "We deny not that there will be more taylors and shoomakers; but there will also be more suits and shoos made than before" – and sold to the immigrants, among others.

The speculative basis of the fear of citizen unemployment is simple: if the number of jobs is fixed and immigrants occupy some jobs, there are fewer available jobs for natives...Immigrants have practically no negative effect in the labor market on any person except other immigrants. The effect on wages is modest by any appraisal, and the effect on unemployment apparently is zero. It is all-important that these facts are agreed upon by all observers. The following pages will be a review of the literature by the editors of a volume on this subject produced by the National Bureau of Economic Research.

Increased immigration has a modest adverse effect on the wages of the immigrants themselves and on the wages of earlier waves of immigrants, but it has only a modest effect on the wages of the young black and Hispanic Americans who are likely to be the next closest substitutes (LaLonde and Topel). Neither the employment nor the wages of less educated black and white natives worsened noticeably in cities where immigrant shares of the population rose in the 1970s. On the positive side, there is some evidence that, in cities with more immigrants, employment grew more rapidly or declined more slowly in low-wage industries where immigrants tended to find jobs and that less skilled natives moved into better jobs (Altonji and Card). The broad implication is that immigrants have been absorbed into the American labor market with little adverse effect on natives (Abowd and Freeman 1992, 2).

VEDDER-GALLAWAY-MOORE HISTORICAL AND CROSS-SECTIONAL STUDY

Vedder et al. (1994) examined the relationship between the rates of unemployment (relative to population) and the rates of unemployment for the United States as a whole during the 20th century. They "found no statistically reliable correlation between the percentage of the population that was foreign-born and the national unemployment rate over the period 1900-1989, or for just the postwar era (1947-89)" (p. A12). They also compared rates across states. In Vedder's words,

Messrs. Gallaway, Moore and I took the 10 states with the highest average percentage of immigrant population in the 1960-90 period and compared them with the 10 states with the smallest relative immigrant presence. In the 10 high-immigrant states, the median unemployment rate in the 1960-91 period was about 5.9%, compared with 6.6% in the 10 low-immigrant states.

Classifying the states according to unemployment rates and confining our analysis to the 1980s leads to even more startling results. We compared the 10 states with the lowest average annual unemployment rates in the years 1980-90 with the 10 states with the highest average annual unemployment rates. The median proportion of the population that was foreign-born was 1.56% in the high-unemployment states, compared with 3.84% in the low-unemployment states. More immigrants, lower unemployment (Vedder et al. 1994, A12).

EFFECTS ON EMPLOYMENT OF THE LESS-SKILLED AND MINORITIES

Muller and Espenshade: Cross Section of Metropolitan Areas

Muller and Espenshade examined black unemployment in 247 metropolitan areas in the United States and 51 metropolitan areas in California, New Mexico, and Arizona (states with large proportions of persons from Mexico)...Black unemployment rates are not increased – if anything, they are lowered – by a rise in the proportion of Mexican immigrants in a local labor market...

Muller and Espenshade also made a special study of the effect of Hispanic immigration upon blacks, the group which they adjudged to be the Hispanics' closest competition in the labor market. They first examined the rates of labor force participation

"I don't know why you're going this way—
You know we can't afford anything in this aisle."

Cartoon by Carol ★ Simpson. Reprinted with permission.

and unemployment for the years 1970, 1980, and 1982, covering a period of heavy immigration within Los Angeles County, with these results:

Blacks generally, and black teenagers especially, do not appear to have been harmed by immigration in the period from 1970 to 1981...An examination of labor force participation data for Los Angeles by sex and race from the 1970 and 1980 censuses indicates that black women had gains that were above the average for them nationwide, while black men experienced a decline that was somewhat lower than the decline for them nationwide. And in 1982, when unemployment in California reached its highest rate in four decades, nonwhite labor force participation rates for both teenagers and adults in the Los Angeles area continued to exceed national rates.

Native workers who find their jobs jeopardized by immigrants may experience higher rates of unemployment, if they do not drop out of the labor force altogether...The period from 1970 to 1982 was marked by rising rates of unemployment, both nationwide and in California. For all groups in the United States, unemployment rates more than doubled. The smallest increases were for blacks in Los Angeles – 27 percent for adults and 35 percent for teenagers – followed by black teenagers in California. In sum, trends in unemployment rates do not provide evidence of sharp job competition between immigrants and blacks (1985, 96-97)...

Muller's Study of Los Angeles

Even the job prospects for black teenagers do not appear to be adversely affected by the influx of immigrants. Total teenage unemployment in Southern California is close to the national average, but unemployment among black teenagers is substantially lower than average (1984, 14)...

THE FIX-PASSEL REVIEW OF EFFECTS ON AGGREGATE EARNINGS

Fix and Passel reviewed the studies concerning the effect of immigration on wages of natives across industries without distinguishing among groups of natives. They summarize as follows: Immigration has no discernible effect on wages overall...Wage growth and decline appear to be unrelated to immigration – a finding that holds for both unskilled and skilled workers (1994, 48).

Here is another summary among many, particularly relevant because it is by George Borjas, an economist whose work is often cited favorably by anti-immigration groups. "The empirical evidence indicates that immigrants only have a minor effect on the earnings and employment opportunities of natives." About illegals in particular, he writes, "There is no evidence...that illegal immigration had a significant adverse effect on the earnings opportunities of any native group, including blacks" (1990, 221, 90)...

LALONDE AND TOPEL ON NATIVES' AND IMMIGRANTS' EARNINGS

LaLonde and Topel studied immigrants' and natives' earnings and education in the 1970 and 1980 U.S. censuses and found that although it is true that immigration has small effects on wages, virtually all of this burden falls on immigrants themselves. Labor market effects for non-immigrants are negligible. Taken together, these results suggest that any adverse effects of current immigra-

IMMIGRATION AND EMPLOYMENT

The principal findings of the study are:

1) In our examination of immigration over the long-term we find no statistical support for the conventional wisdom that increased immigration leads to higher unemployment. Periods of heavy immigration are not associated with subsequent higher than normal unemployment...

In fact, we find that the ten states with the lowest concentrations of immigrants in 1980 had a typical unemployment rate that was nearly one third higher than in the states with relatively high immigration...

These findings flatly contradict the common assertion that new immigration restrictions will improve national labor conditions or those within heavily impacted states such as California and New York. The evidence suggests that immigrants create at least as many jobs as they take, and that their presence should not be feared by U.S. workers...

Immigrants may contribute to the job creation process in several ways. First, immigrants may expand the demand for goods and services through their consumption. Second, immigrants may contribute to output through the investment of savings they bring with them. Third, immigrants have high rates of entrepreneurship which may lead to the creation of new jobs for U.S. workers. Fourth, immigrants may fill vital niches in the low and high skilled ends of the labor market, thus creating subsidiary job opportunities for Americans. Fifth, immigrants may contribute to economies of scale in production and the growth of markets. Proponents of this perspective would argue that the combined effect of these five points is such that immigration will not cause unemployment, and indeed might even lead to its decline...

We find no reliable evidence that immigration causes unemployment...If anything, unemployment seemed to be negatively associated with immigration: more immigrants, less unemployment. In short, the evidence does not suggest that immigration causes unemployment. A much stronger case, indeed, can be made from the results that immigration may actually reduce joblessness, but the most judicious and objective interpretation of the findings is that "immigration does not have much impact on the rate of unemployment."

Stephen Moore, Lowell Gallaway and Richard Vedder, "Immigration and Unemployment: New Evidence," Alexis de Tocqueville Institution Position Paper, March, 1994.

tion flows on the U.S. labor market and on native welfare will be small (LaLonde and Topel, 1991, 302)...

It is often argued that blacks are the one group whose economic progress is most likely to be hampered by the entry of immigrants into the United States. Perhaps the most surprising insight provided by the recent evidence is that no study finds any evidence to support this claim...

Recent research, therefore, has not been able to establish a single instance in which the increase in the supply of immigrants had a significant adverse impact on the earnings of natives (1990, 86-88). ...the entry of Mexican-born illegal aliens barely affects the earnings of natives. A 10-percent increase in the size of the Mexican illegal-alien population reduces the earnings of Mexican-American men by .1 percent; does not change the earnings of black men; reduces the earnings of other men by .1 percent; and increases the earnings of women by .2 percent. There is no evidence, therefore, to suggest that illegal immigration had a significant adverse impact on the earnings opportunities of any native group, including blacks (1990, 90)...

EFFECTS ON WAGES OF MINORITIES AND THE POOR

Fix and Passel Summary of Effects on African-Americans

Immigration has no negative impacts for black workers taken as a whole, according to the evidence. But less skilled black workers and black workers in high immigration areas with stagnant economies are negatively affected. Given the far higher unemployment rates of African-American males than white males, it is not surprising that this is one of the most frequently examined issues in the economics of immigration and benefits from the most recent research. Particular findings that inform this issue include:

Native African-Americans in areas of high immigration fared better than native African-Americans in low-immigration areas in terms of wage and employment growth. In high-immigration areas, however, native African-American wages do not keep pace with the rising wage trends that immigration brings for Anglos and Hispanics (Enchategui 1993).

Immigrants increase the labor market opportunities of African-Americans in strong local economies but reduce them where labor demand is weak (Bean, Fossett, and Park 1993). Thus, increased immigration may hurt African-Americans in recessionary periods and help them in periods of growth. This finding qualifies the results of two studies of high-immigration regions – New Jersey (Espenshade 1993) and Miami (Card 1990) – which found no effects...

SELF-EMPLOYMENT

Considering the entire stock of immigrants in the United States as of 1980, Borjas (1990, 165) found that they are slightly more likely to be self-employed than natives – 12.2 percent to 11.4 percent. And those who are self-employed make slightly more money than self-employed natives (a modest interpretation indicates no meaningful differences.) To the extent that self-employed persons create jobs for others, these numbers suggest that immigrants create jobs in similar proportion to the extent to which they fill jobs. This in part explains how it can be that a larger number of immigrants does not imply increased unemployment among natives.

RECOGNIZING AUTHOR'S POINT OF VIEW

This activity may be used as an individualized study guide for students in libraries and resource centers or as a discussion catalyst in small group and classroom discussions.

Many readers are unaware that written material usually expresses an opinion or bias. The capacity to recognize an author's point of view is an essential reading skill. The skill to read with insight and understanding involves the ability to detect different kinds of opinions or bias. **Sex bias, race bias, ethnocentric bias, political bias,** and **religious bias** are five basic kinds of opinions expressed in editorials and all literature that attempts to persuade. They are briefly defined below.

Five Kinds of Editorial Opinion or Bias

- **Sex Bias** – The expression of dislike for and/or feeling of superiority over the opposite sex or a particular sexual minority.

- **Race Bias** – The expression of dislike for and/or feeling of superiority over a racial group.

- **Ethnocentric Bias** – The expression of a belief that one's own group, race, religion, culture, or nation is superior. Ethnocentric persons judge others by their own standards and values.

- **Political Bias** – The expression of political opinions and attitudes about domestic or foreign affairs.

- **Religious Bias** – The expression of a religious belief or attitude.

Guidelines

1. Locate three examples of **political opinion** or **bias** in the readings from Chapter Three.

2. Locate five sentences that provide examples of any kind of **editorial opinion** or **bias** from the readings in Chapter Three.

3. Write down the above sentences and determine what kind of bias each sentence represents. Is it **sex bias, race bias, ethnocentric bias, political bias** or **religious bias?**

4. Make up one-sentence statements that would be an example of each of the following: **sex bias, race bias, ethnocentric bias, political bias** and **religious bias.**

5. See if you can locate five sentences that are factual statements from the readings in Chapter Three.

Summarize author's point of view in one sentence for each of the following readings:

Reading 10 _____

Reading 11 _____

Reading 12 _____

Reading 13 _____

Reading 14 _____

CHAPTER 4

RESTRICTING IMMIGRATION

READING

15

PREVENTING CONFLICT AND CHAOS

Pat Buchanan

Pat Buchanan is a conservative columnist, syndicated nationally. He has bid for the Republican nomination for the Presidency twice.

■ **POINTS TO CONSIDER**

1. What will the United States look like demographically in 2050, according to forecasts?

2. Describe the consequences of continued "relaxed" immigration policy, as Buchanan views them.

3. Discuss Buchanan's proposal for immigration. How will this proposal allow the nation to "fix the broken melting pot?"

Pat Buchanan, "We Need to Call a Time-Out on Immigration," **Conservative Chronicle**, 11 September 1994: 10. © **Tribune Media Services**, Inc. Reprinted with permission.

Unlike 20 years ago, ethnic conflict is today on almost every front page.

Proposition 187 "is an outrage. It is unconstitutional. It is nativist. It is racist" – Al Hunt, Capital Gang, CNN. That outburst by my columnist colleague, about California's Prop. 187 – which would cut off social welfare benefits to illegal aliens – suggests that this savage quarrel is about more than just money. Indeed, the roots of this dispute over Prop. 187 are grounded in the warring ideas that we Americans hold about the deepest, most divisive issues of our time: ethnicity, nation, culture.

SHAPING THE NATION'S CHARACTER

What do we want the America of the years 2000, 2020 and 2050 to be like? Do we have the right to shape the character of the country our grandchildren will live in? Or is that to be decided by whoever, outside America, decides to come here? By 2050, we are instructed by the chancellor of the University of California at Berkeley, Chang Lin-Tin, "the majority of Americans will trace their roots to Latin America, Africa, Asia, the Middle East and Pacific Islands."

Now, any man or woman, of any nation or ancestry, can come here – and become a good American. We know that from our history. But by my arithmetic, the chancellor is saying that Hispanics, Asians and Africans will increase their present number of 65 million by at least 100 million in 60 years, a population growth larger than all of Mexico today.

What will that mean for America? Well, south Texas and southern California will be almost exclusively Hispanic. Each will have tens of millions of people whose linguistic, historic and cultural roots are in Mexico. Like eastern Ukraine, where 10 million Russian-speaking "Ukrainians" now look impatiently to Moscow, not Kiev, as their cultural capital, America could see, in a decade, demands for Quebec-like status for southern California. Already there is a rumbling among militants for outright secession. A sea of Mexican flags was prominent in that L.A. rally against Prop. 187, and Mexican officials are openly urging their kinsmen in California to vote it down.

If no cutoff is imposed on social benefits for those who breach our borders, and break our laws, the message will go out to a des-

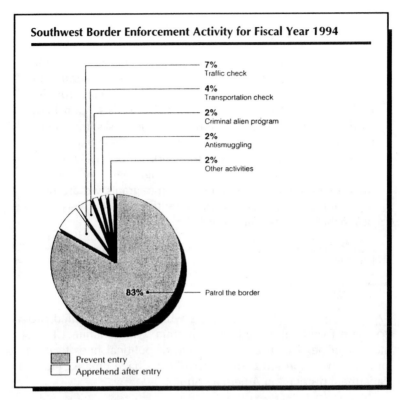

Southwest Border Enforcement Activity for Fiscal Year 1994

7%
Traffic check

4%
Transportation check

2%
Criminal alien program

2%
Antismuggling

2%
Other activities

83% — Patrol the border

Prevent entry
Apprehend after entry

Source: GAO analysis of INS data.

perate world: America is wide open. All you need do is get there, and get in.

REAPING THE CONSEQUENCES

Consequences will ensue. Crowding together immigrant and minority populations in our major cities must bring greater conflict. We saw that in the 1992 L.A. riot. Blacks and Hispanics have lately collided in D.C.'s Adams-Morgan neighborhood, supposedly the most tolerant and progressive section of Washington. The issue: bilingual education. Unlike 20 years ago, ethnic conflict is today on almost every front page.

Before Chancellor Chang's vision is realized, the U.S. will have at least two official languages. Today's steady out-migration of

"Anglos" or "Euro-Americans," as whites are now called, from southern Florida and southern California, will continue. The 50 states will need constant re-drawing of political lines to insure proportional representation. Already we have created the first "apartheid districts" in America's South.

A MELTING POT TO REPAIR

Ethnic militancy and solidarity are on the rise in the United States; the old institutions of assimilation are not doing their work as they once did; the Melting Pot is in need of repair. On campuses we hear demands for separate dorms, eating rooms, clubs, etc., by black, white, Hispanic and Asian students. If this is where the campus is headed, where are our cities going?

If America is to survive as "one nation, one people," we need to call a "time-out" on immigration, to assimilate the tens of millions who have lately arrived. We need to get to know one another, to live together, to learn together America's language, history, culture and traditions of tolerance, to become a new national family, before we add a hundred million more. And we need soon to bring down the curtain on this idea of hyphenated-Americanism.

If we lack the courage to make the decisions – as to what our country will look like in 2050 – others will make those decisions

IMMIGRATION SOARS

The Immigration and Naturalization Service (INS) projected that overall legal immigration levels would jump from last
year's 720,000 to about 935,000 this year. And nearly all of
the swell will be coming from the wildly permissive "family
reunification" program – which allows recent immigrants to
bring in numerous relatives without regard to skill or education. Admissions in this program will jump from 593,000 to
835,000.

"INS Says Legal Immigration Is Now Soaring by 41%," **Human Events**, 10
May 1996.

for us, not all of whom share our love of the America that seems
to be fading away.

READING

16

RECYCLING THE GOSPEL OF EUGENICS

Peter A. Quinn

Peter A. Quinn is the author of the novel, Banished Children of Eve *(Viking, 1994). The following comments were excerpted from an article in* America *Magazine.*

■ POINTS TO CONSIDER

1. Discuss the eugenics movement. What brought about its conception and acceptance?

2. How did the Irish immigrants of the 1840s differ from migrant waves past and present?

3. Describe the response of Anglo societies to the Irish.

4. Compare and contrast immigration sentiment today with that of the past.

Peter A. Quinn, "Closet Full of Bones," **America**, 18 February 1995: 10-13. Reprinted with the permission of Peter A. Quinn and America Press, Inc., 106 West 56th Street, New York, NY 10019. Originally published in **America's** February 18, 1995 issue.

The fear that white civilization is growing steadily weaker and is at risk of being overwhelmed by barbarians from within and without marks a new life for an old and ugly tradition.

A specter is haunting the West: immigration. From the passage of Proposition 187 in California to the growing anti-immigrant movements in Europe, there is a widespread attempt by economically advanced societies to seal themselves off from the less fortunate. The imagery used to describe these immigrants is almost always the same: Immigrants are to hordes what sheep are to flocks, or lions to prides. They swarm rather than arrive, their faceless uniformity evoking the insect world and its ceaseless, relentless capacity to reproduce...

THE GOSPEL OF EUGENICS

The fear that white civilization is growing steadily weaker and is at risk of being overwhelmed by barbarians from within and without marks a new life for an old and ugly tradition. The most infamous manifestation of that tradition is the Ku Klux Klan and the host of so-called Aryan resistance groups that continue to spring up on the periphery of American political life. But its most powerful and enduring effect was not limited to cross-burnings or rabble-rousing assaults against blacks and immigrants. There was a far more respectable, educated version of this tradition that clothed itself in the language of science and not only won a place in the academy, but helped shape our laws on immigration, interracial marriage and compulsory sterilization of the mentally ill and retarded.

The movement derived its authority from the work of an Englishman, Francis Galton – Darwin's cousin – who in 1883 published his masterwork, *Inquiries into Human Faculty and Its Development...* In it Galton advocated the modification and improvement of human species through selective breeding and coined a name for it as well: *eugenics.* In Galton's view, which was shared by many of his Victorian contemporaries and buttressed by a wealth of pseudo-scientific skull measuring and brain weighing, the races were totally distinct. Eugenics, he believed, would give "the more suitable races or strains of blood a better chance of prevailing speedily over the less suitable."

SOUTHERN AND EASTERN EUROPEAN INFLUX

At the turn of the 20th century, the United States was ripe for the gospel of eugenics. The country's original immigrants – Anglo-Saxon and Scots-Irish Protestants – were feeling battered and besieged by the waves of newcomers from southern and eastern Europe (i.e., Italians, Slovaks and Ashkenazi Jews) who were judged so immiscible in appearance and conduct that they would undermine the country's character and identity. According to the eugenicists, the racial "germ plasm" of these groups was riddled with hereditary proclivities to feeblemindedness, criminality and pauperism. These suspicions were given scientific justification by studies that purported to trace family behavior across several generations and discern a clear pattern of inherited behavior.

By the eve of World War I, eugenics was taught in many colleges. Its research arm was generously funded by some of America's wealthiest families, including the Harrimans, Rockefellers and Carnegies. Alfred Ploetz, the German apostle of "racial hygiene," hailed the United States as a "bold leader in the realm of eugenics," a leadership that consisted of the widespread ban on interracial marriage and the growing emphasis on compulsory sterilization.

In the wake of the First World War, the eugenicists helped direct the campaign to halt the "degeneration" of the country's racial stock by changing its immigration laws. As framed by Henry Fairfield Osborn, the president of the Museum of Natural History (at that time a center of eugenic fervor), America would either stop the influx from southern and eastern Europe or it would perish: "Apart from the spiritual, moral and political invasion of alienism, the practical question of day by day competition between the original American and the alien element turns upon the struggle for existence between the Americans and aliens whose actions are controlled by entirely different standards of living and morals."

The eugenicists played an important role in achieving the Immigration Restriction Act of 1924, a victory noted and approved by Adolf Hitler in his book of the same year, *Mein Kampf*. In fact, nine years later, when the Nazis took power in Germany, they would hail U.S. laws on immigration, intermarriage and sterilization as models for their own legislation.

Cartoon by Carol ★ Simpson. Reprinted with permission.

THE IRISH AND IMMIGRATION

As successful as the eugenicist crusade was, it was not the first time that the United States had experienced a broad and widely supported campaign against the influx of intractable foreigners whose essential alienism – their alleged lack of moral or mental stamina – would, it was believed, eat away the foundations of American democracy and sink the country into a permanent state of pauperism.

The country's first great immigrant trauma (that is, aside from the forced importation of African slaves) began 150 years ago, in

1845, with the failure of the potato crop in Ireland and the onset of a catastrophe that would result in the death of a million Irish from hunger and disease, and force millions to flee. "The volume of Famine emigration," writes historian Kirby Miller, "was astonishing: between 1845 and 1855 almost 1.5 million sailed to the United States...In all, over 2.1 million Irish – about one-fourth of Ireland's pre-Famine population – went overseas; more people left Ireland in just eleven years than during the preceding two and one-half centuries."

The flight of the Irish Famine produced an immigrant experience unlike any other in American history. There was no web of emigration societies or government agencies to encourage or cushion the process of resettlement abroad. In effect, traditional Irish society – the life of the townslands and the rudimentary agriculture that supported the mass of the Irish tenantry – came apart, dissolving into a chaotic rout. Faced with the simple choice of flee or starve, or in many cases left by eviction with no choice at all, the Irish abandoned the land.

From Liverpool to Boston, contemporary observers remarked on the utter destitution of the Irish who poured into their streets, many of them ill and emaciated and, in the words of one eyewitness, "steeped to all appearances in as hopeless barbarism as the aboriginal inhabitants of Australia."

The dislocation that resulted was enormous. Although the memory of what happened has been softened by the romantic haze that obscures much of our true immigrant history, the passage of the Irish Famine was stark and bitter. Their arrival was the major impetus to the growth of the largest third-party movement in American history, the American or Know-Nothing Party, which was predicated on a loathing for Catholics in general and Irish ones in particular. In the popular mind, the Irish became identified with poverty, disease and violence, a connection strengthened by events like the New York City Draft Riots of 1863, the worst urban uprising ever to occur in the United States. The scale of social turmoil that followed the Irish into America's cities would not be seen again for another century, until the massive exodus of African-Americans from the rural south to the urban north.

Today the sense of the Catholic Irish as wholly alien to white, Christian society seems, perhaps, difficult to credit. But in the mid-19th-century America the inalterable otherness of the Irish was for many a given...

BUBBLING THEORIES OF RACIAL INFERIORITY

Although eugenics was still a generation away, the theory of Irish racial inferiority was already being discussed. In 1860, Charles Kingsley, English clergyman and professor of modern history at Cambridge University, described the peasants he saw during his travels in Ireland in Darwinian terms: "I am daunted by the human chimpanzees I saw along that hundred miles of horrible country...to see white chimpanzees is dreadful; if they were black, one would not feel it so much, but their skins, except where tanned by exposure, are as white as ours"...

The migration of the rural poor was, is and will always be problematic. But the challenges it presents can only be aggravated by doomsday fearmongering that casts the issue in terms of a vast and imminent "Volkerwanderung" (wandering) in which the wretched of the earth will infest and overrun Western civilization.

Writing in 1866, Charles Wenworth Dilke recorded his journey across America, Africa and much of Asia. A recent university graduate with high political ambitions, Dilke saw the world caught up in the struggle of light and dark. He framed the future in terms of the competition for survival between the "dear races" (Europeans of Teutonic origin) and the "cheap races" (the hordes of Irish, Indians, Chinese, etc.). For Dilke, "the gradual extinction of the inferior races" was not only desirable but would be "a blessing for mankind."

Dilke was a lofty-minded imperialist. Though contemptuous of other cultures and a racial alarmist, he was no proponent of geno-

119

cide. Yet we know the kind of final solutions these vicious and simplistic scenarios of racial struggle and survival can lend themselves to. Maybe the Victorians did not. We do.

LESSONS OF OUR PAST

We need to remind ourselves that immigrants are not a single genus. They come in all shapes and sizes. They have immense strengths and talents as well as liabilities. Their potential for enriching and enlivening the societies that receive them is every bit as real as the difficulties their presence can create.

Certainly, those of us who descend from the Famine Irish would seem to have a special responsibility to look past the current evocation of innumerable, anonymous hordes threatening our borders, or the latter-day recycling of theories of ethnic and racial inferiority, and to see in the faces of today's immigrants the image of our ancestors: those hungry ghosts who, though dispossessed and despised, passed on to us their faith and their hope.

READING

17

VICTORY IN CALIFORNIA

Justin Raimondo

Justin Raimondo wrote the following for The Free Market, *the publication of the Ludwig von Mises Institute. The Ludwig von Mises Institute is a conservative institute of policy studies in Auburn, Alabama.*

■ POINTS TO CONSIDER

1. Summarize the author's description of California Proposition 187.

2. According to Raimondo, describe the political divisions for Proposition 187 and explain why they exist.

3. Discuss the predictions of Proposition 187's opponents.

4. Were there any odd political partnerships in the Proposition 187 debate? Explain.

Justin Raimondo, "Victory in California," **The Free Market**, January, 1995: 1, 6-7.
Reprinted by permission.

The biggest shock, to people who heard about Proposition 187 for the first time, was to discover that illegals could become welfare bums with the full backing of the law.

The two-to-one vote in favor of California's Proposition 187 is a milestone in the battle against the welfare state. It is a victory that will help reclaim individual liberty against centralized power. Out-spent, smeared, and attacked by both Left and Right, grass-roots activists put Prop. 187 over the top. The story of their triumph is an object lesson in how exploited American taxpayers can take back the liberty and property the ruling political class has systematically stolen from them for more than a century.

The opinion-making elites were in a state of virtual hysteria in the months before election day. Fearful of the burgeoning nation-wide rebellion against government that all the polls foretold, they were especially terrified that Californians might pass the initiative.

WHAT IS PROPOSITION 187?

What exactly did the referendum propose? It brought an end to all government subsidies to illegal aliens in California, including welfare in the form of public education and health care, except in cases of emergencies. That's it. It was a chance, perhaps for the first time this century, for the people of a state to vote on whether to keep or scrap a welfare program in its totality.

Let's be clear: Prop. 187 did not attack immigration. Immigration policy, however flawed, is set in Washington and remains unchanged. It did not even crack down on illegal immigration; the initiative said nothing about deporting or arresting illegals who come to live and work in the private sector. Illegals can attend any private school that will take them, or educate their children at home, as more and more citizens are doing anyway.

MISGUIDED OPPOSITION

The sole focus of Prop. 187 was forbidding non-citizens from looting the citizens of California. Even people who favor more immigration should have rallied behind 187; it would insure that people who come here intend to work. Even people who champion illegal immigration could have favored Prop. 187; it insured that illegals would not be leaching off the citizenry.

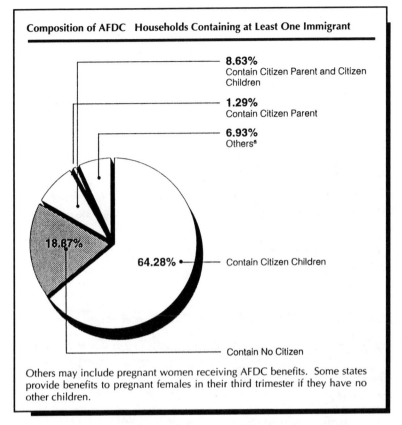

Composition of AFDC Households Containing at Least One Immigrant

8.63%
Contain Citizen Parent and Citizen Children

1.29%
Contain Citizen Parent

6.93%
Others[a]

18.87%

64.28% — Contain Citizen Children

Contain No Citizen

Others may include pregnant women receiving AFDC benefits. Some states provide benefits to pregnant females in their third trimester if they have no other children.

Source: Department of Health and Human Services, 1993.

As documented by George Borjas, the welfare participation rate of immigrants has doubled since 1970. In California, the costs in tax dollars approached the stratosphere. Illegals comprised 7% of the state's total student population, and cost $2 billion per year for education. California would have to build up a new 600-student school every day for five years just to keep up with the illegal population.

California's health care costs for illegals run $1 billion per year...Even a moderate Republican like Pete Wilson knew something had to be done. He tried to end this policy at the state level, but ran up against the central government's objections. In violation of California's rights, the feds were forcing state taxpayers to pay up whether they liked it or not. Gov. Wilson even took out full-page ads in the *Washington Post* asking the federal government to give the state a break, but to no avail. It was then that fed-up citizens took matters into their own hands.

OUR POLITICAL DECLINE

It is a measure of the decline of our official political culture that Prop. 187 would even have to be debated – or, for that matter, would have to be brought up at all. In fact, the biggest shock, to people who heard about Prop. 187 for the first time, was to discover that illegals could become welfare bums with the full backing of the law.

When initiative proponents gathered enough signatures to get Prop. 187 on the ballot, the establishment was horrified. For here was a popular proposal that not only rolled back the welfare state, but also represented a chance for voters to clarify the purpose of government, which is not to redistribute citizens' wealth to non-citizens.

The usual suspects shifted into high gear, including government employees, teacher unions, labor unions, big business, civil rights lobbies, "public interest" law firms, doctors, government hospital employees, big universities, and establishment politicians. Most of them, of course, had something to gain from expansion of the welfare state.

First, they trained all their guns on the woefully under-funded, politically inexperienced grassroots activists in the "Yes on 187" committee. These activists were called every name in the book, as the smear brigade went into overdrive. This well-funded opposition even ran radio ads claiming that 187 was backed by "white supremacists."

Reporters were insane with anger, dropping all pretenses at journalistic "objectivity." And every major editorial page in the state denounced the initiative. So did the *Wall Street Journal*, the *New York Times*, and the *Washington Post*.

SCARE TACTICS

Then came the scare campaign. Every sort of horror, from epidemics of tuberculosis to outbreaks of crime and organized rioting, were trotted out as the inevitable consequence of the initiative's passage. Illegals themselves threatened the end of civil society. In the end, however, none of it worked, and California's voters put a stop to the most objectionable form of welfarism imaginable.

Once passed, a federal judge in Los Angeles used the tyrannical power of his office to override the verdict of California's voters. If Prop. 187 is eventually declared "unconstitutional," it will tell us what's wrong with judicial tyranny, not the initiative. It would also signal an agenda for the future.

But it wasn't just the Left and the Establishment that mobilized against Proposition 187. Some intellectuals, politicians, and think tanks of the respectable Right launched a frantic campaign as well. Canadian commentator David Frum and Washington neoconservative William Kristol joined the attacks. And one week before the election, Cesar V. Conda of the Alexis de Tocqueville Institution gathered signers for a statement opposing Prop. 187. "In our view," the statement said, missing the point entirely, the initiative will become "a hostile crusade against all immigrants."

He gathered signers from most of the big think tanks, including the Heritage Foundation, the Reason Foundation, the Cato Institute, the Manhattan Institute, and the Competitive Enterprise Institute. The media reported that these groups had thrown their institutional weight into defeating the measure.

JACK KEMP AND WILLIAM BENNETT

The antics of Jack Kemp and Bill Bennett made the Tocqueville Institution statement appear moderate, however. To media cheers, they echoed the message of their liberal allies. Put simply, they said Prop. 187 is racist. "Does anyone seriously doubt that Latino children named Rodriguez would be more likely to appear to be illegal than Anglo children named, say, Jones?"

125

To begin with, according to the text of Prop. 187, all students signing up for tax-funded education would be asked to provide proof of citizenship, whether their name is Rodriguez, Kemp, or Bennett. And since Kemp and Bennett assert that asking school-children to provide proof of citizenship smacks of "totalitarianism," then why isn't asking them for proof of residence, routine medical records, and even their names – normal procedure in all schools, both public and private – a violation of their "civil liberties?"

To argue that putting restrictions on welfare provision is a "government intrusion" is like saying people on Social Security shouldn't have to prove their age. Other conservative opponents claimed that Prop. 187 would lead to a "national identity card." Again, the initiative merely said that those who choose to go on welfare in one form or another in the state of California must provide proof that they are citizens. There is nothing ominous about providing proof of citizenship. And if this discourages people from going on welfare, that's the purpose.

The Washington and New York conservatives could have remained neutral, which itself would have been suspect. Instead, they attempted to defeat a measure ending welfare. In effect, they came out for perpetually increasing spending for non-citizens. In effect, this is the same as lobbying for confiscatory taxation and redistribution to benefit people who are here illegally.

EVEN CONSERVATIVES HIDE THE TRUTH

But how, you ask, could any ostensible conservative spin out such a rationale for continuing subsidies, especially to non-citizens? Easy: they don't tell the truth. "We want to be clear and emphatic on this point," said Bennett and Kemp, "we are not in favor of illegal immigrants receiving state or federal welfare benefits."

But a memo dated June 22, 1988, and signed by Jack Kemp during his tenure as HUD Secretary, says the opposite. In response to concerns raised by citizens of Costa Mesa, California, over a HUD-funded hiring hall that catered to illegals, Kemp wrote: "HUD's community development programs do not require citizenship or lawful resident status for eligibility. It is the presumption that the programs benefit both citizens and documented and undocumented aliens." We are furthermore told, in Kemp's best hectoring style, that distinguishing among recipients "on the basis of alienage would be discriminatory"...

Besides this glorious victory against the welfare state, the Prop. 187 battle clarified the dividing line between Washington and New York conservatives, who flinched when it mattered, and the real right at the grassroots, which is anti-welfare, anti-regulation, anti-central state, and free market to the core. If the spirit of Prop. 187 is to thrive and grow, it will have to depend on the tenacity of independent minds and voices.

READING

18

MISTREATING ALIENS IN OUR MIDST

Aaron Gallegos

Aaron Gallegos wrote the following commentary for Sojourners *Magazine, an evangelical Christian journal of political, social, and moral controversy.*

■ **POINTS TO CONSIDER**

1. According to Gallegos, what sentiments do initiatives like Proposition 187 generate?

2. Discuss Proposition 187's potential "quality of life" effects.

3. What hypocrisy does the author feel is revealed by support for anti-immigrant initiatives?

4. Summarize the potential long-term burdens on society if measures like Proposition 187 spread across the country, according to the author.

Aaron Gallegos, "Room in the Inn?" **Sojourners**, December, 1994/January, 1995: 10-11. Reprinted by permission, **Sojourners**, 2401 15th Street N.W., Washington, D.C. 20009; (202) 328-8842 or (800) 714-7474.

The proponents' campaign showed just whose families they value the most and that their self-righteous zeal stops fast at the border of race and class.

Though California's anti-immigrant Proposition 187 is new, the spirit behind it is not. While the Jewish people were living as exiles in Babylon, the self-promoting, power-hungry Haman stirred up the people against them. "There is a certain people scattered...in all the provinces of your kingdom," he said to the king. "Their laws are different from those of all other people...so it is not in the king's interest to let them remain" (Esther 3:8).

Similar to Haman's invective against the Jews in Babylon two-and-a-half millennium ago, the passage of Proposition 187 in California stokes the nativist wildfire that is sweeping the country. It seems, as backers had hoped, that Proposition 187 will spur a re-examination of the 1982 Plyler v. Doe Supreme Court decision, when the court ruled that states could not bar immigrant children from public schools. Even though civil rights groups have filed numerous lawsuits challenging 187 and California judges have blocked its implementation until the legal controversy is resolved, its victory by a 3-to-2 margin sends a strong anti-immigrant message to Washington and the rest of the country.

Proposition 187 would exclude undocumented immigrants from welfare benefits and all but emergency health care (even immunization against contagious diseases), ban the children of illegal immigrants – whether these children were U.S. citizens or not – from public schools, and mandate educators and medical providers to deny services to persons "reasonably suspect" of being undocumented. But since illegal immigrants were already ineligible for most public assistance in California, the initiative in reality strikes hardest at their children – who are the poorest and most vulnerable segment of the state's population.

WHOSE FAMILY VALUES?

Ironically, the primary proponents of 187 were many of the same conservatives that are leading the so-called family values push in the state. Their campaign showed just whose families they value the most and that their self-righteous zeal stops fast at the border of race and class. In a miscarriage of justice that the biblical prophets would have mocked, Gov. Herod's...er, Wilson's first step in enforcing 187 was to order that pregnant

129

"It's simple really. If you FLOAT, we give you amnesty. If you SINK, we deport you."

Cartoon by Carol ★ Simpson. Reprinted with permission.

women who are undocumented immediately be denied access to state-provided prenatal care. The Latino Christmas tradition of *posada*, in which a couple dressed up as Mary and Joseph go from house to house in the barrio looking for a place that will welcome them, may be all too real for immigrants in California this season.

It is also ironic that in an election where the country voted overwhelmingly against big government and public spending, Californian voters should choose a measure whose enforcement will require a huge state bureaucracy. Though California voters were motivated to "take back the state" by cutting the amount the state spends on social services for illegal immigrants, it is unlikely that 187 will either save much money once it is actually imple-

PROPOSITION FOR DISASTER

Disastrous social consequences flow from depriving children of education: underemployment and greater marginalization, leaving these children no motive for or means of fitting into society. Gangs then beckon as an alternative means of survival.

Nor is there any legitimate connection between the costs of providing medical care to immigrants and the legality of their status as citizens or resident aliens. Proposition 187 presents serious difficulties in terms of public health. Bacteria and viruses distribute themselves without regard for national borders or the status of their carriers as citizens or aliens. If an undocumented alien is carrying an infectious or contagious disease, to leave it untreated foolishly risks spreading it to other citizens.

Edward McGlynn Gaffney, Jr., "Immigrant Bashing," **Christian Century,** 1 Mar. 1995.

mented or stop the flow of undocumented immigrants into the state.

Modern immigrants – like most of our ancestors – do not come into this country to join welfare roles but to seek a better life for themselves and their children, which means, in most cases, the opportunity to work. Proposition 187 hurts the quality of life in California, not only for illegal immigrants, but for all the residents of the state. If 187 succeeds in throwing the children of illegal immigrants out of the schools, the wider society will have to bear the long-term burden of young people who are going without an education or competitive job skills.

ANTI-IMMIGRANT SENTIMENT IS HERE AGAIN

The proposition also has influenced people from all sectors of California – as well as in other parts of the United States – to look at those who speak with an accent, whose skin is any color but white, or who have a "foreign-sounding" surname (which, depending on your definition of foreign, most of us do) as criminals and the cause of local economic woes. The Orwellian character of Proposition 187 threatens to turn California's schools and

ANTI-IMMIGRANT SENTIMENT SPANS NATION

After the passage of Proposition 187, California has bequeathed its anti-immigrant rhetoric to the rest of the nation. House Republicans leapfrog over one another to see who can come up with the most restrictive legislation; Senate Republicans and Democrats aren't far behind. Proposals range from a 30 percent reduction to an all-out moratorium on the number of immigrants to be allowed legally into the country.

Ruben Martinez, "One Year After Proposition 187, California's Undocumented Speak Softly But Carry a Big Mop," **Star Tribune**, 23 Oct. 1995.

medical facilities into vigilante immigration offices and encourages children to turn in their undocumented parents.

Proposition 187 represents yet another turn of anti-immigrant, racist scapegoating that has risen many times before in our history, usually in times of economic stagnation. Yet there are those from every sector of the population who are able to see beyond the borders of divisive politicking and view increasing diversity as a concrete benefit to the country and the economy – a perspective supported by history.

The initiative spurred the formation of multiracial coalitions that launched protests before and after the election which got many people – especially young Latinos – out into the streets for the first time. "We are seeing the birth of a new Latino civil rights movement here, and the issue is going to be the rights of non-citizens." Latino advocate Antonio Gonzalez told *The Los Angeles Times*.

The astounding demographic changes that this country has seen in the last decade have prompted those with the most to lose to gather their forces for a last-ditch effort to retain control over the future of the country. Yet it isn't diversity that will cause the feared balkanization of this country, but the attitude of disrespect and intolerance that measures like 187 promote. Uncontrolled immigration into the United States needs to be better regulated than it is now, but the way to do this isn't to pass laws that attack the poor as they struggle for their chance in this land of opportunity.

A SHORTAGE OF FARM WORKERS

James S. Holt

James S. Holt is an agricultural economist. He is senior economist for the management labor law firm McGuiness and Williams, and the Employment Policy Foundation in Washington, D.C.

■ POINTS TO CONSIDER

1. Summarize the reasons Holt gives for a shortage of resident migrant labor.

2. How much of the migrant farm worker force is illegally in the country? According to the author, why would restrictions on illegals not affect the wages of legal farm labor?

3. What determines the "price of labor" in the market for these types of farm commodities?

4. Discuss what the author believes would result if restrictions on illegal labor were enforced.

Excerpted from the testimony of James S. Holt before the Subcommittee on Immigration and Claims of the House Judiciary Committee, December 7, 1995.

Because aliens are already a significant portion of the U.S. seasonal agricultural work force, reducing the supply of seasonal agricultural labor will have little or no impact on employment and wages for U.S. farm workers.

The public policy issue before the Congress is whether a workable program for admission of temporary and seasonal agricultural labor is in the national interest as an integral part of the reform of illegal immigration. How will such a policy impact domestic farm workers, other domestic workers (including farmers) in agriculture and related industries, the level of domestic economic activity, U.S. trade, and, of course, our ability to control illegal immigration? All these important questions are interrelated.

A LARGE AND RAPIDLY GROWING SECTOR OF AGRICULTURE

With rising incomes worldwide, and changes in consumers' tastes and preferences favoring fruits and vegetables, the demand for labor-intensive agricultural commodities is growing rapidly. United States agricultural producers have participated in that growth. The 1992 United States Census of Agriculture reported that fruits, vegetables and horticultural specialties accounted for more than $23 billion of agricultural sales in 1992, a 32 percent increase from that reported in the previous agricultural census five years earlier. Most economists expect demand for labor-intensive agricultural commodities to continue a strong growth pattern.

Although there is no hard evidence for this, many agricultural economists agree that the availability of labor, especially alien labor illegally entering the United States, has been an important factor facilitating the growth in U.S. labor-intensive agricultural production. The U.S. has, in fact, had a *de facto* alien worker program, albeit one that was uncontrolled and unregulated. As protection of labor-intensive commodities has expanded, the expansion has undoubtedly been in areas of well-suited land resources where the available labor supply had limited expansion and in areas more remote from available domestic labor supplies. Such production could only develop if there was a supply of seasonal labor willing to migrate into the area to perform the seasonal labor-intensive tasks. Seasonal alien migration, including many illegal entrants, met that need.

134

Until recently, U.S. domestic producers of labor-intensive commodities, especially fresh commodities, were relatively protected from foreign competition in the U.S. domestic market by the difficulty and high cost of shipping perishable commodities. Export markets for these commodities were limited by these factors, and by an extensive array of trade restrictions and protective barriers. Both the technological constraints and trade barriers to international competition in labor-intensive agricultural commodities have fallen away in recent years, and freer trade is clearly a continuing trend. This has increased competition from foreign producers in domestic markets, but has also opened up opportunities for U.S. producers in export markets. An increasing proportion of the expansion in labor-intensive agriculture in the United States is for the export market.

GROWTH HAS CREATED TENS OF THOUSANDS OF JOBS

The public policy debate on temporary alien agricultural workers often focuses only on the occupations in which aliens are employed, and overlooks the fact that although some seasonal manual field jobs may be held by aliens, employment in labor-intensive agriculture, and employment created by labor-intensive agricultural production, extends far beyond these manual field jobs. Policy analysis should properly take into account all the employment affected by the policy.

According to USDA statistics, farming accounted for only 1.1 percent of U.S. gross domestic product (GDP) and about 1.6 percent of total U.S. employment in 1992. However, the food and fiber sector accounted for 15.7 percent of GDP, and 18 percent of total employment. Farming is only one part of the interrelated linkage of industries that comprise the food and fiber sector, but it is the engine that drives the economic activity and employment in a significant portion of that sector.

Farmers purchase inputs and services to carry out agricultural production from so-called "upstream" industries. USDA estimates that every dollar of GDP generated by farming creates an additional dollar of GDP in upstream activities. Farmers sell products to "downstream" industries. These industries transport, pack, process, store, manufacture, distribute, retail, consume or export farm products. USDA estimates that about eight dollars of U.S. GDP in downstream activity is generated by every dollar of GDP generated in farming. And the importance of these upstream and downstream activities is growing. USDA estimates that inputs purchased by farmers increased 95 percent in real terms and downstream activities increased by 87 percent in real terms between the early 1960s and the early 1980s.

Total employment in the food and fiber sector accounts for 18 percent of U.S. employment. Some components of this employment would be relatively unaffected by a shift in market share of production from U.S. to foreign producers, namely employment in wholesale and retail trade and foodservice. But approximately 40 percent of food and fiber sector employment, or 8 percent of total U.S. employment, is potentially affected by where farming production takes place. Put another way, about three jobs outside of farming are dependent on each job in farming. A shift in production of farm commodities from U.S. to foreign producers will not only eliminate farm jobs, but on average about three times as many non-farm jobs.

Data from studies indicate that the proportion of undocumented workers has increased by about 4 to 5 percentage points annually since 1989. This is roughly consistent with a Commission on Agricultural Workers estimate of "an annual increase of unauthorized worker in the order of approximately 6 percent."

An effective system for verifying employment authorization combined with effective enforcement of employer sanctions, will significantly reduce the supply of temporary and seasonal labor for U.S. agriculture.

U.S. WORKERS CANNOT REPLACE ALIEN LABOR

Won't growers be forced to raise wage offers to domestic farm workers and U.S. residents not now employed to attract additional labor in the absence of aliens? This, of course, is the rationale for many people's opposition to a temporary foreign worker program, and is at the core of the public policy question raised by "guest worker" programs. If the answer to that question were "yes" we would have the best of all possible worlds. Growers could continue in production, more U.S. residents would be employed and farm worker wages would be higher. Unfortunately, however, the answer to the question is "no". Both economic theory and the real world tell us that.

THE NEED TO FILL WORK

Our goal is not to displace U.S. workers by bringing in "guest workers." We will hire any local people who are willing and able to do this work. Anyone who has operated a farm or processing facility in Georgia knows that you cannot function without migrant labor. There is not an adequate local labor force to keep our businesses running. There are a variety of reasons local laborers are not lining up for jobs. This is probably not the forum for that discussion but it, too, should be addressed.

I ask you today to establish an adequate Guest Worker Program that will allow us to have a legal supply of labor to continue to operate our farms.

Excerpted from the testimony of Robert Dasher, Vidalia Onion Business Council, before a joint hearing of the Subcommittees on Risk Management and Specialty Crops; and Immigration and Claims of the House Judiciary Committee, December 14, 1995.

First it is useful to review the data on farm wage rates. Contrary to common perception, farm work is not minimum wage work. USDA reported the U.S. 1994 average hourly earnings for non-supervisory field workers was $6.02 per hour. For workers paid by piece rate, U.S. average hourly earnings were $7.02 per hour. When they are working, the weekly hours of farm workers are generally comparable to those of non-farm workers. For example, in California, where one quarter of all the field workers in the Nation are employed, the 1994 average hourly earnings for non-supervisory field workers was $6.51 and the average hours of work per week (for those who were working) was 41.5 hours.

Then why don't minimum wage workers abandon their jobs and do farm work at a 40 percent raise? The answer undoubtedly lies in the other characteristics of seasonal farm work. Seasonality itself is foremost among these. While field work pays relatively well on the average when there is work, it is by definition seasonal. Most U.S. workers need and prefer more reliable year round work, and many are obviously willing to take less per hour in order to secure more stability of employment. A second unattractive feature of agricultural work is that many jobs entail physical labor under adverse environmental conditions of heat, cold, sun, rain, etc. It is work that many Americans would be physically incapable of doing on a sustained basis, and that most of the rest would prefer not to do if there are better alternatives available. Thirdly, and in my view probably the most important factor, is that many seasonal farm jobs are not located within normal commuting distance of most workers. In order to take these jobs workers have to become temporary migrant farm workers. Although there is no data to substantiate this, I believe that this is especially characteristic of the areas where expansion in production of labor-intensive commodities has more recently occurred. Not only have we stigmatized migrant farm work in this country; we have spent literally billions of dollars of public money trying to reduce domestic migrancy and "settle out" migrant farm workers. It is not surprising, therefore, that there is a "shortage" of willing U.S. migrant farm workers. Aliens, on the other hand, are willing to migrate, in fact are required to do so to get into the United States.

This should not leave you with the impression that U.S. residents will not do farm work. In fact, the best available data shows that more than 2 million U.S. residents currently do hired farm work at some time during the year. The problem that we are discussing here is that because of the availability of alien labor, first under circumstances where it was not illegal for employers to employ these aliens, and more recently possessing documents that employers are legally obligated to accept, U.S. agricultural production has expanded beyond the capacity for the U.S. resident work force to meet its needs. That expansion has, of course, been beneficial to the U.S. It has expanded U.S. economic activity and created additional jobs for U.S. residents. But it has left U.S. agriculture dependent on an alien labor supply.

ECONOMIC IMPACT OF A REDUCTION IN LABOR

Economic theory demonstrates that reducing access to alien labor will only increase domestic farm worker wages in a closed economy. In an economy open with free trade such as exists in the United States, the domestic farm wage and employment level is established by world market prices. Reducing access to alien labor will reduce U.S. producers' world market share, but will leave U.S. farm worker employment and wages largely unaffected.

138

The central public policy argument for a legal program for the continued admission and employment of aliens in seasonal agricultural jobs in the U.S. is that the availability of alien labor expands U.S. employment. Because aliens are already a significant portion of the U.S. seasonal agricultural work force, reducing the supply of seasonal agricultural labor to U.S. producers will reduce U.S. production of labor-intensive agricultural commodities and shift market shares for these commodities from U.S. to foreign producers. It will have little or no impact on employment and wages for U.S. farm workers. The reduction in U.S. production of labor-intensive agricultural commodities will, however, reduce derivative employment for U.S. workers in farming and in upstream and downstream agribusiness occupations. Thus the alternatives confronting policymakers in evaluating a guest worker program for U.S. agriculture do not involve weighing benefits to one group of U.S. residents (U.S. farmers and agribusiness workers) against costs to another group of U.S. residents (U.S. farmworkers). The "costs" of restricting the labor supply to U.S. agriculture will fall on U.S. farmers and U.S. workers in allied industries. The "benefits" of restricting the U.S. seasonal agricultural labor supply will accrue largely to producers and workers outside the U.S.

In other words, in the absence of trade restrictions or direct legislation, government policy cannot affect domestic farm worker wage levels, which are established by world prices for similar commodities delivered into U.S. markets.

READING

20

A SURPLUS OF RURAL LABOR

Robert A. Williams

Robert A. Williams made the following comments in his capacity as an attorney with Florida Rural Legal Services, Inc.

■ POINTS TO CONSIDER

1. Is there a shortage of legal farm labor, according to Williams?

2. What is responsible for the unemployment or underemployment of legal farm workers, in the author's view?

3. How should Congress respond to industry demands to increase or relax foreign farm labor in the U.S.?

4. Describe how agribusiness has, in William's view, used government programs to perpetuate the farm worker surplus.

Excerpted from the testimony of Robert A. Williams before the Subcommittee on Immigration and Claims of the House Judiciary Committee, December 7, 1995.

Agribusiness is rewarded for failing to improve its labor practices.

First and foremost, there is no farm worker shortage in the U.S. as the growers themselves have admitted. Since the passage of the Immigration Reform and Control Act of 1986 (IRCA), study after study has shown that there is a surplus of workers in agriculture. Last year, as in years past, approximately 1.6 million farm workers filled several million short-term seasonal jobs in agriculture.

If there were a shortage, simple economics tells us that wages would have risen as employers bid up the price of labor. Unfortunately, since the mid 1980s, there has been little incentive for employers to increase benefits or improve working conditions for farm workers. Wages and working conditions have stagnated or actually deteriorated, according to both the Commission on Agricultural Workers and Department of Labor's (DOL) National Agricultural Worker Survey. Recently, tomato pickers in Immokalee, Florida, were protesting yet another paycut. Wages for citrus workers in Southwest Florida have also fallen since 1990 despite the fact that more workers have been needed each year as new groves come into production.

If there were a shortage, one would expect to see changes in farming practices to employ fewer workers, either by increased mechanization or switching to less labor-intensive crops. Instead, there has been a significant expansion of labor-intensive fruit, vegetable, and horticultural specialty production in the United States.

EMPLOYER SANCTIONS WON'T WORK

I understand that the growers' position is that while there may not be a shortage of labor now, there would be if there was an effective system for verifying employment authorization combined with effective enforcement of employer sanctions. I remain skeptical that these two conditions will ever be met; in my twenty-year experience working with farm workers I have yet to see any employment law that was effectively enforced in the agricultural setting. There are over 10,000 farm labor contractors in the United States with nearly a 20 percent turnover every year. They have proven impossible for DOL to regulate. As long as the grower is allowed to hide behind them, there is little hope that employer sanctions can be effective in agriculture. Therefore a new guest worker program would not substitute a legal work force for an illegal work force as the growers claim, but would simply add to the labor surplus and further worsen the situation of the permanent residents and citizens who comprise the majority of the farm labor work force in the United States.

U.S. WORKERS ARE AVAILABLE TO FILL ANY SHORTAGE

The growers contend that there are no U.S. workers available to fill the needed jobs if our country gets serious about removing illegal aliens from the workforce. But the overwhelming evidence shows widespread pervasive underemployment and unemployment among farm workers. If growers need legal workers, they can go to their local Job Service office. Last year, over 70,000 farm workers who registered for work at Job Service offices throughout the nation were not referred to any job. In fact, 44 percent of all farm worker applicants are unable to obtain a job referral through the Job Service. Another 25,000 farm workers were referred to jobs, but not placed in a job. All of these workers were U.S. citizens or legal residents of the United States.

Unemployment appears to be most persistent in the very areas where the growers claim they cannot find a legal work force. For example, in 17 major agricultural labor-use counties in California, during the period from December 1986 to the present, unemployment has rarely been less than 10 percent during the peak harvest periods or less than 15 percent during the off-peak months. The total number of rural unemployed in these counties has actually gone up during the last ten years. There are also many unemployed people who are not farm workers who would be available to do farm work jobs. Last year, the U.S. Employment Service placed almost as many non-farm workers in short-term agricultural jobs as it did farm workers. Over 42,000 non-farm workers were placed in short-term agricultural jobs through the Job Service.

THE GROWERS ALREADY HAVE A FOREIGN WORKER PROGRAM

Finally, the growers' demands for a foreign worker program ignores the fact that there is already one in existence – the H-2A program, a program which is rife with abuses of both domestic and foreign workers. Bad as the H-2A program is, the growers apparently want a program with no protections at all for domestic workers. The H-2A program's requirements are neither burdensome nor unreasonable. For example, housing for H-2A workers generally must meet the minimal standards set by Occupational Safety and Health Administration (OSHA). A bare room measuring seven feet by eight feet with a steel prison bed and mattress, a bare bulb overhead and a concrete floor is all that an H-2A employer need provide. Far from having extensive legal protections, H-2A workers are excluded from the major federal statute which protects U.S. farm workers, the Migrant and Seasonal Agricultural Worker Protection Act. Any additional costs associated with the use of H-2A workers are more than offset by savings resulting from not having to pay payroll taxes on foreign workers. Growers claim that the H-2A program is unworkable, yet for those who are in the H-2A program, the program has worked all too well; year after year, these growers have had their applications for workers granted by DOL without making any real effort to recruit U.S. workers. Only very rarely are the H-2A employers denied foreign workers. For them, a supposedly temporary solution to a short-term labor shortage has become a permanent way of life.

The key feature of the growers' proposal is to replace the current labor certification with an attestation procedure similar to that used in the H-1B program. This proposal would cede control of the nation's borders to the industry most responsible for the continued flow of illegal immigrants into this country. Under the growers' proposal, no one at DOL would even check to see that the foreign workers were filling jobs for which no U.S. workers could be found or that such workers were being paid the prevailing wage.

CONCLUSION

The fatal flaw shared by all temporary foreign worker programs in agriculture is that the worker is not "free to choose." We all recognize that what keeps working conditions high for most Americans is not federal bureaucrats or even well-intentioned legal services attorneys, but the ability to go across the street and look for a better job if our present employer does not offer a fair day's pay for a fair day's work. The temporary foreign worker can't do that, and when Congress enacts these programs, it takes away that freedom from Americans too – because now if a U.S. worker is dissatisfied with the terms of employment cooked up by some industry consultant and approved by a DOL bureaucrat, he either must accept them or see the job go to a foreign worker.

Once again, agribusiness is asking to be rewarded for failing to improve its labor practices. While other U.S. employers have tried to comply with the Immigration Reform and Control Act of 1986, agribusiness has continued to rely on a continued flow of unauthorized workers.

Like the boy who murdered his parents and pled for sympathy on the grounds that he was an orphan, agribusiness has the *chutzpah* to argue for yet another foreign worker program based on the facts that the working conditions for its workers are so bad that no American who had any choice would ever take the job and that consequently it has continued to blatantly violate the law against employing illegal immigrants. The clear alternative to a continued reliance on an alien workforce in agriculture, is for Congress to "just say no" and for agribusiness to begin to compete with other employers for a U.S. work force by finally offering decent wages and working conditions.

READING

21

ADMITTING REFUGEES: POINTS AND COUNTERPOINTS

John L. Martin v. Bill Frelick

John L. Martin wrote the following statement for the Center for Immigration Studies, a non-profit, non-partisan research organization that examines the economic, social and demographic impact of immigration. Bill Frelick is Senior Policy Analyst for the U.S. Committee for Refugees, a non-profit, non-governmental organization which defends the rights of refugees and asylum seekers. Both authors discuss the proposal to limit refugees into the U.S. to 50,000 annually.

■ POINTS TO CONSIDER

1. Summarize the problem of refugees and asylum seekers as outlined by both authors.

2. Why does Martin believe the nation should cap the number of asylum seekers and refugees who enter the U.S.? Upon what does he base his cap number?

3. According to Frelick, why is the cap on refugees unwise?

4. What has traditionally determined the flow of refugees to the U.S.?

Excerpted from John L. Martin, "Reducing Legal Immigration," Center for Immigration Studies Backgrounder, September, 1993. Reprinted by permission. Also excerpted from Congressional testimony by Bill Frelick before the House Committee on the Judiciary, June 29, 1995.

JOHN L. MARTIN: THE POINT

When the Refugee Act was adopted in 1980, it was contemplated that refugee immigration from all sources would not be over 50,000 per year. Many of the entrants under the asylum provision are abusers of the process and rightfully considered illegal immigrants rather than refugees. These numbers hopefully will drop as a result of current reform efforts.

Refugee newcomers today tend most often to be from the Third World. Over eighty percent of the refugees in the resettlement program were from East Asia. Only about five percent were from Europe. The current refugees are less likely to bring education and work skills that will facilitate a quick transition to self-support and, unlike earlier periods of refugee flows from Europe, they are less likely to have relatives to join. They, therefore, are more likely to become a burden on the taxpayer, frequently at the state and local level when federal transition funding runs out.

The United States accepts more refugees for resettlement – by far – than any other country. Yet our program represents only a drop in the bucket compared to U.N. estimates of 18 million refugees in the world today. We have been generous in accepting refugees from areas where we have been militarily involved, e.g., Southeast Asia. For example, last year's immigration statistics include Amer-Asian children who have been admitted as if they were refugees, even though they are not. Cuba and the former Soviet bloc have been other sources of major intake. Because of the rapid, profound political changes taking place around the world in the post-Cold War environment, it would seem that this program should be reviewed with the objective of attempting to establish a firm ceiling to entries on a non-discriminatory basis. A major reduction from current entry levels would not require a change in the law, only an agreement between the legislative and executive branches.

There are good reasons why such a reduction might, in fact, be in the best interest of refugees. The first has to do with the refugee resettlement program in the United States. Not all those who would like to be settled in the United States can be, so our focus should be on how to make sure that those who are accepted are given the best chance for a successful transition to a new life in this country. The other reason relates to a focus on those who cannot be resettled in the United States and how we might best focus our assistance to do the most to help them survive their period as refugees until they can be resettled in their home country.

Because there is currently no firm ceiling on refugee admissions and the decision-making process on intake levels is divorced from the process of funding transitional support programs for the new refugees, the federal funding level to support the settlement and adjustment of the refugee influx has not kept pace. This has meant that the funding level per refugee has been consistently decreasing. If the number of refugees were scaled back to the 50,000 level contemplated in the 1980 legislation, for example, the funding level would not run out before the refugees have had a chance to learn English and workplace skills that are intended to prepare them to become self-supporting. Such a change would also diminish the current inequitable impact of the refugee program on the states that receive the largest numbers, e.g., California and Florida. At present, when the federal support funds are exhausted after eight months (rather than the three years originally contemplated in the legislation), the states are left holding the bag for support services paid out of state funds.

With the knowledge that the vast majority of refugees will never be resettled in the United States or elsewhere, the United Nations and others have called for an allocation of scarce refugee funding to be channeled to the basic shelter and feeding needs of the refugees in UN-run camps as near as possible to their home countries. When conditions permit, the refugees are then assisted by the UN in repatriation programs to return home. Since the bulk of refugees come from Third World countries and seek refuge in neighboring Third World countries, there is no doubt that international resources can stretch farther in support programs if directed toward these United Nations programs. That is the thrust of a recommendation by a recent Trilateral Commission report on refugees authored by Doris Meissner, the Immigration Service Commissioner-designate.

To achieve and maintain a reduction, Congress must set an unbreachable ceiling on refugee and asylee resettlement. Otherwise the combined special pleadings for exceptional treatment will lead to an ever-expanding admissions policy, as experience with the 1980 Refugee Act has demonstrated.

BILL FRELICK: THE COUNTERPOINT

H.R. 1915 would limit the annual admission of refugees to 75,000 in FY 1997 and 50,000 thereafter. The 50,000 limit could be exceeded only if Congress enacts a law to that effect, or, under existing law, if the President determines that an unforeseen refugee emergency exists. The rationale for this provision appears to be the 1980 Refugee Act's establishment of 50,000 as the "normal flow" of refugees to be resettled in the U.S., and the fact that admissions during the 15 years since the Act have exceeded that level.

The 50,000 "normal" admissions level was calculated simply by dividing the number of refugees admitted during the 1970s by ten. However, the average during the course of a decade did not reflect the ebb and flow of refugee movements during that time. Admissions went from 146,000 in 1975 to 27,000 the next year, back up to 111,000 in 1979, reflecting primarily the Southeast Asian caseloads. In the next decade, admissions ranged from a high of 207,000 in 1980 to a low of 67,000 in 1986, reflecting not only the continuing flows from Southeast Asia but also the wars in Afghanistan and Ethiopia, the on-again, off-again manipulation of the freedom of movement by Communist governments from Havana to Moscow, the collapse of the former Soviet Union, and new crises elsewhere in the aftermath of the Cold War.

Worldwide, the number of persons classified as refugees has risen by nearly seven million in the last ten years, to the current sixteen million.

By their very nature, refugee movements are not susceptible to "normal flows." The desire to "manage" refugee flows, to make them amenable to bureaucratic planning and immigration preferences, sacrifices the imperative to protect the most vulnerable in favor of political and bureaucratic expediency. Imposing a 50,000 cap on annual refugee admissions would make our refugee program less flexible and less responsive to refugee protection. While it is true that the U.S. refugee admissions program is discretionary and that the U.S. government can and does choose how many refugees to admit on an annual basis, and it can operate this program in as orderly and predictable a fashion as it likes, irrespective of the worldwide need, the reality is that refugee crises are neither orderly nor predictable, and that any country wishing to respond meaningfully to these crises must be flexible.

Even with the unpredictability of situations that create refugees, the admissions program does require some planning, including the establishment of worldwide and regional admissions ceilings. Under current law, these ceilings are set by the President each year, based on current data from refugee processing posts and U.S. political and financial concerns. Although the Southeast Asia program is now in a phase-down mode, and many hope that the refugee admissions needs for minorities from the former Soviet Union might decline after several more years, there is no certainty whatsoever that Russian and other former Soviet states will overcome centuries of anti-semitism and intolerance for other minorities in the coming years. In fact, recent evidence of hypernationalism, political disarray, and brutal repression of Muslims in Chechnya suggest that the situation there could become considerably more dangerous. In any case, the United States remains strongly committed to continuing both the former Soviet and Southeast Asian resettlement programs for the immediate future, for reasons that serve U.S. interests and Congressional mandates.

The United States is not just any country. We are the world's remaining super power. Beyond power, we also claim to promote standards of humanity and human rights for the world as a whole. Regardless of what we say, our world leadership is fundamentally determined by our actions. And our actions with respect to refugees and asylum seekers are a litmus test of our moral authority to speak on human rights generally.

That authority has been eroded in recent years, most especially by our policy concerning the interdiction and summary return of Haitian boat people between mid-1992 and mid-1994. That policy seriously undermined the international consensus, built during the four previous decades, to provide asylum seekers with an opportunity to make their claims and to protect refugees from forced return to persecution. We are slowly repairing some of the damage of that policy.

Lowering the number of refugee admissions and setting limits on refugee admissions would not only make our admissions program less flexible and responsive, but would also indicate to other potential resettlement countries a lessening in our commitment to refugee resettlement as a durable solution on behalf of refugees who cannot return home. Continuing to seek ways to block asylum seekers from access to asylum procedures not only leaves those persons affected unprotected, but also sends a signal to other countries with less capacity to assist refugees and less well-established traditions of due process that it is permissible to keep asylum seekers at arm's length and to insulate them from legal protections. With no government willing to provide them a venue for safety, the victims of human rights abuse may find themselves without the possibility of escape and without protection.

SECURING INTERNATIONAL BOUNDARIES

Duncan Hunter

Duncan Hunter is a representative in the House from the State of California.

■ POINTS TO CONSIDER

1. What does the author believe is the most effective way to stop illegal immigration, and why?

2. Discuss the difficulties with patrolling the border between the U.S. and Mexico.

3. Describe the changes made in the border patrol in different experimental projects.

4. According to the author, have experimental border patrol step-up operations had success? If so, discuss these successes.

Excerpted from the testimony of Duncan Hunter before the Subcommittee on Immigration and Claims of the House Judiciary Committee, March 10, 1995.

I believe our first and foremost task must be to seal off our borders to illegal entrants.

In recent years, I have worked with Republicans and Democrats alike, to find legislative solutions to our border problems. The complex nature of our generous immigration laws and the difficulty of enforcing them has created a public outcry for an overhaul of the system. Yet amidst the discussion over the importance of restricting federal benefits to illegals, enforcing employer sanctions, or reforming the asylum process, I have come to the conclusion that there is no substitute for a secure border.

SECURING THE BORDER

Understanding the importance of a comprehensive reform effort, I believe our first and foremost task must be to seal off our borders to illegal entrants. I have long advocated a large increase in the Border Patrol, whose main duty is to control the vast areas between the ports of entry. Until recently, this critical agency was chronically underfunded, resulting in an undermanned and ill-equipped interdiction team. Their duties include not only capturing illegal aliens and alien smugglers, but also interdicting the massive amounts of narcotics that attempt to enter between the ports. In the desert portion of my district, where illegal alien crossings are relatively low, it is estimated that over 70% of California's cocaine supply is trafficked through the region each year. Despite the best efforts of the Border Patrol and record seizures by agents, they are fighting a losing battle against an increasingly mobilized and well-armed narcotics industry.

In June of 1993, I successfully added an amendment to the Commerce, Justice, State and the Judiciary Appropriations bill for 600 additional Border Patrol agents. The amendment passed overwhelmingly – although against the wishes of the subcommittee chairman. The following year, I worked with the same coalition of members to add a similar number of agents during the appropriations process, and to authorize 6,000 additional Border Patrolmen in the Violent Crime Control and Law Enforcement Act of 1994.

As a result of the budgetary increases, the Immigration and Naturalization Service (INS) placed more agents in high traffic sectors, however, questions have arisen in regard to the agency's recent tactics. Following the success of Operation Hold the Line in El Paso, where 400 of the sector's 650 agents were deployed on a 24-hour per day, 7-day per week basis along the 20-mile metropolitan corridor, the INS pledged to replicate this operation in varying forms along the Southwest border. This strategy is clearly superior to the cat and mouse games that agents were forced to play due to insufficient resources, and was endorsed by a majority of the Members of Congress representing our border with Mexico.

OPERATION GATEKEEPER

Operation Gatekeeper in the San Diego sector is the second major blockade undertaken on the Southwest border. This initiative utilizes three tiers of agents allowing aliens and smugglers to cross the international line in an attempt to apprehend a majority of them within a mile of the border. The INS believed this strategy of "guaranteed apprehension" would deter future crossers as word filtered back to Mexico. Since October of 1994 when Gatekeeper began, apprehensions decreased significantly, though not as much as the INS expected. In succeeding months, apprehensions took a sharp increase, as the traditional post-holiday crossers felt undeterred by the new operation. Aside from comments by the INS' own personnel that Operation Gatekeeper is not working to their expectations, the strategy of maintaining fallback positions is under sharp criticism from the General Accounting Office, as evidenced in their new report on border control. During a recent interview, Jim Blume, an official with the General Accounting Office, stated: "Our position is that illegal aliens shouldn't be allowed to cross the border and enter U.S. territory...they should be prevented from crossing the border."

This statement is also echoed in a study conducted by Sandia National Laboratories entitled "Systematic Analysis of the Southwest Border." Working through the INS, Sandia Labs analyzed all nine southwest sectors and came up with serious arguments against the old apprehension tactics and in favor of a visible Border Patrol presence on the line. Among their suggestions are the construction of multiple barriers in high-traffic urban areas, augmented by lights and patrol roads; and the placement of agents directly on the border to impose "effective barriers on the free flow of traffic." This clearly reflects my philosophy and that of the other Members who helped secure additional resources for the Border Patrol, yet this is not the approach undertaken by the INS thus far.

SECURING OUR NATION'S BORDERS

We are a state and a nation of immigrants, proud of our immigrant traditions. Like many of you, I'm the grandchild of immigrants. My grandmother came to this country in steerage from Ireland at age 16. She came for the same reason any immigrant comes – for a better future than she could hope for in the old country. And America benefited from her and millions like her.

But we, as a sovereign nation, have a right and an obligation to determine how and when people come into our country. We are a nation of laws, and people who seek to be a part of this great nation must do so according to the law.

Pete Wilson, "Securing Our Nation's Borders, **Vital Speeches**, 25 Apr. 1994.

UNWILLINGNESS TO CONFRONT CRISIS

Arguments that the El Paso operation cannot be replicated in San Diego due to logistical problems signal an unwillingness to address the crisis at hand. While the possibility of violence in response to a blockade is a clear threat, there are numerous ways to mitigate proximity to illegal crossers while maintaining a visible presence as an effective deterrent. As an example, El Paso has the natural barrier of the Rio Grande River, yet in many portions of the San Diego sector, reinforced fencing serves as a similar impediment. Proximity to illegal crossers can be further buffered in San Diego through the installation of secondary, chain-link fencing with patrol roads in between. This allows for the continued restriction of any drive-through traffic, and maintains a visible link between agents and crossers on foot. The Sandia study proposes a similar barrier system, underscoring the need for deterrence rather than interdiction.

The benefits of a secure border are clear and irrefutable. Following initial protests over the El Paso operation, border crime and automobile thefts in the metropolitan area dropped markedly. The relationship between Border Patrol agents and the community improved as agents focused on securing the border area rather than patrolling the city looking for aliens and smugglers. Even in San Diego, following initial protests against the reinforced fencing, assaults on border patrol agents plummeted and the number of border murders dropped to zero in one year. The strategy stopped drive-through traffic forcing drug and alien smugglers east to other, less fortified sectors. With the forward deployment of the Border Patrol, we could all but halt illegal foot traffic in San Diego – and in other sectors as well.

The recent surge in apprehensions in the Arizona sectors underscores the need for a comprehensive effort to secure the entire border. Slow and piecemeal approaches to staunch the illegal flow in selected areas serve only to allow drug and alien smugglers the time and opportunity to find other avenues of entry. In the meantime, we will continue to spend exorbitant amounts of taxpayer dollars detaining, feeding and shuttling captured aliens back and forth to the border. Although border enforcement will not solve all of the immigration-related problems we face, I believe it must be our first step in this process, reaffirming the federal government's responsibility and commitment to securing our international boundaries.

READING

23

MILITARIZING THE BORDER

Carlos Hamann

Carlos Hamann wrote the following article for the National Catholic Reporter (NCR). NCR *is an independent Catholic newsweekly based in Kansas City, Missouri.*

■ **POINTS TO CONSIDER**

1. Why has crossing the Mexico/U.S. border become attractive to middle-class Mexicans?

2. How has the border crackdown affected the availability of illegal migrant labor in the U.S.?

3. How has Bill Clinton's Administration dealt with the border issue?

4. Discuss why those cited in the article do not feel crackdown measures will stop the flow of illegal immigrants.

5. Describe the problems with the Mexican economy.

Carlos Hamann, "Fences, Patrols Can't Stem Tide of Eager Mexicans," **National Catholic Reporter**, 5 Apr. 1996. Reprinted by permission, **National Catholic Reporter**, Kansas City, MO. Subscriptions: (800) 333-7373.

Agents overseeing immigration control have started to point to a need for economic changes in Mexico rather than border crackdowns as a more effective way of curbing immigration.

Every night hundreds of men, women and children gather on the international boundary line separating the United States from Mexico, just south of the remote town of Douglas, Arizona. Pushed from their homes by Mexico's collapsing economy and pulled by the prospect of a menial job in the United States, these travelers spend the night trying to bolt past a phalanx of U.S. Border Patrol agents and make it to the relative safety of a larger, more anonymous U.S. city. Success would mean landing a job washing dishes at a restaurant, sewing shirts at a garment sweatshop, harvesting California produce or mowing lawns for minimum wage or less, with scanty benefits and little access to U.S. government relief programs.

Welcome to the latest target in the 1996 90-day border crackdown on immigrants. This special $2.6 million operation, which began Jan. 16, sent 200 extra Border Patrol agents and 100 Immigration and Naturalization Service (INS) officers to the busiest crossing points along the border with Mexico to help local agents who claim they are overwhelmed by new swells of people venturing north.

"Before, we'd get groups of three or four trying to cross the border," said Border Patrol agent Alfredo Esquivel, who has been in Douglas since December 1994. "Now we're seeing groups of 50 or 60. We're also encountering a lot of families."

MIDDLE-CLASS MIGRANTS

Along with increasing numbers, there are some other unexpected twists in the illegal immigration picture. Agents overseeing immigration control have started to point to a need for economic changes in Mexico rather than border crackdowns as a more effective way of curbing immigration. More middle-class Mexicans are migrating than before; apparently even some professionals are finding it difficult to make an adequate living at home since the country's economy collapsed.

Both Douglas and its Mexican sister city, Agua Prieta, are in the middle of a pancake-flat, sagebrush desert 120 miles southwest of Tucson, the nearest large city. The towns have never before been an important crossing point for undocumented migrants. In 1995, the INS reported that half of all undocumented immigrants living in the United States entered legally; when their visas expire, they are left without papers. Historically, about half of the people crossing the U.S.-Mexico border without visas entered at San Diego, Nogales, Ariz. (one hour south of Tucson), and El Paso, Texas. But since patrols intensified, the flow of migrants has shifted to isolated towns like Douglas.

It is this mobility and the persistence of immigrant travelers, Border Patrol agents say, that render repressive, anti-immigration policies ineffective. Esquivel, for example, recently stopped 10 men attempting to cross the border at an area called "the jungle," a thicket of thorny bushes, tall weeds and cacti. His flashlight penetrating their hiding place in the brush, Esquivel told the men calmly in Spanish, "Don't worry, you don't need to run."

After frisking the men, the agents decided none appeared to be trafficking drugs or working as "coyotes," contractors who smuggle other immigrants through. Such suspicions would lead to a computer fingerprint check at the local immigration office. These men, however, were simply asked to sign a single-page voluntary repatriation document, which none of them read, and Border Patrol agents escorted them back to the border.

Esquivel shrugged at the futility of the evening's work: "They'll probably be back in an hour." In two months alone, agents in Douglas repatriated an estimated 34,500 migrants like these men – more than twice the town's population of 14,000. The statistics, however, can be deceptive. Many migrants will continue to try to cross the border regardless of how many times they're caught or how long it takes them to dodge past the Border Patrol. A person caught repeatedly in San Diego, Yuma, Ariz., Nogales and later in Douglas might be counted five or 10 times.

LURED FOR LABOR

The incentive to obtain safe passage – the steady demand for cheap labor in the United States – lures people back, time and again, said Fred Krissman, an expert on immigration from the University of California, San Diego. California's $20 billion-a-year agriculture industry, for example, employs 900,000 farmhands annually to harvest oranges, strawberries, cotton and lettuce. Few of the unemployed in the United States are attracted to these seasonal jobs: They pay poorly and working conditions in the fields are miserable.

A turnover rate of 65 percent fuels the continuous demand for more migrant labor, Krissman said. Even agribusiness leaders recognized the significance of undocumented labor to the industry during December 1995 Senate and House subcommittee hearings on agriculture, he added.

Krissman said the border crackdown has not cut into the availability of farmhands ready to work in California agriculture. "The reality is that immigration authorities need to put on a show at the border, but it's business as usual in the fields," Krissman said. "We can continue to pretend that we're keeping them out, but as long as we don't go after the restaurants, hotels and farm labor contractors that hire them, nothing's going to change."

The political dividends of the "show" and of other anti-immigrant measures are considerable, however. For example, Samuel Schmidt, a Mexico specialist who follows immigration issues from the University of Texas, El Paso, links the successful re-election of California Gov. Pete Wilson in 1994 to his strategy of blaming undocumented migrants for the region's economic malaise.

Following the Wilson victory, President Bill Clinton and the Democratic Party operatives realized that immigration would be a hot topic during the 1995 election campaign, Schmidt said. Since Clinton took office, the INS budget has increased substantially – 72 percent, in fact, from a 1993 total of $1.5 billion to a proposed $2.6 billion for fiscal year 1996.

Those numbers and the recent labor crackdown may give the Clinton campaign a needed boost among one constituency of swing voters, Schmidt said. "No one can attack Clinton for being soft on immigration," he added.

FUTILE CRACKDOWN

As some politicians seek political capital from the immigration debate, agents along the border have begun to doubt the effectiveness of the crackdowns. A recent report on deaths from border crossings released by the American Friends Service Committee (AFSC) claim INS agents in the field "acknowledge the futility of measures designed to make the crossing more difficult."

BORDER HYPOCRISY

Ironically, the Clinton administration, which has voiced the rhetoric of inclusion and appreciation for immigrants, is presiding over the largest militarization of the border between the U.S. and Mexico in modern history.

David Bacon, "Does the Border Have to Feel Like Bosnia?" **Z Magazine**, Mar., 1996.

Both interviews and the AFSC report revealed that many Border Patrol agents are shifting their conversations to economics. In Douglas, for example several agents talked about conditions of poverty in Mexico, admitting that the influx of migrants will continue until employment opportunities and the quality of life improve across the border.

An agent in El Paso agreed. "These people are going to keep coming here (illegally) until the economy improves in Mexico," Steve Pena said. "It's sad. You sympathize with them, but you've got to turn them back. If they want to come to the United States, they have to do it legally."

What about Pat Buchanan's 2,000-mile-long wall? A couple of Douglas agents stopped short of ridiculing the proposal, whose price tag ranges from $45 billion to $167 billion. "We don't need a 2,000-mile-long fence," said former El Paso Border Patrol chief Silvestre Reyes, trying to be polite. "Some of this stuff coming out is to generate political repercussions more than anything else." Reyes ought to know: He designed Operation Hold the Line, a strategy that lined up agents on the busiest section of his border around the clock in El Paso back in September 1993. Hold the Line was used as the model for all current control tactics in border towns. Chances that economic conditions in Mexico that feed immigration will improve soon are slim.

ECONOMIC CHAOS BROADENS

Mexico's economy has been in a tailspin since December 1994 when the peso was devalued by 40 percent. Since then, yearly inflation has jumped from 7 to 52 percent; 1 million jobs have been lost; sales taxes have risen from 10 to 15 percent; the price of electricity has increased 20 percent and gasoline prices have risen 35 percent. Estimates of unemployment range from a government figure of 6 percent to a calculation of 30 percent by the Mexican Workers' Confederation, the country's largest labor union.

Middle-class Mexicans had a rude awakening in 1995 when interest rates on their mortgages, auto loans and credit card debt soared into triple digits. Analysts claim bankers were more interested in attracting foreign investors with the mind-boggling rates than worrying about the impact on the middle class. Interest rates have since dropped to around 70 percent, but middle-class families have not recuperated; bankruptcies are at an all-time high.

Back at the border, a man with a thin mustache stopped by the Border Patrol with several other travelers provided a living example of Mexico's deepening economic chaos. The man, who appeared to be in his 30s, said he was an engineer with a degree from Mexico's Politécnico National University. He said he alone provides for eight family members – his wife, his parents and in-laws and his own children: a baby of six months, an eight-year-old and a teenager.

"Even I have to come here looking for work. There is nothing in Mexico," the engineer said. "Tell your readers they need our labor to harvest your crops. We are not here to steal, just to work." A Border Patrol agent, speaking shaky Spanish, began to question him. Noticing the language barrier, the man responded to the agent's queries in solid English. Meanwhile, another man from the state of Michoacan, in southern Mexico, shrugged. "They got us this time, but we will try 50 times more."

INTERPRETING EDITORIAL CARTOONS

This activity may be used as an individualized study guide for students in libraries and resource centers or as a discussion catalyst in small group and classroom discussions.

Although cartoons are usually humorous, the main intent of most political cartoonists is not to entertain. Cartoons express serious social comment about important issues. Using graphic and visual arts, the cartoonist expresses opinions and attitudes. By employing an entertaining and often light-hearted visual format, cartoonists may have as much or more impact on national and world issues as editorial and syndicated columnists.

Points to Consider

1. Examine the cartoon on page 55.

2. How would you describe the message of the cartoon? Try to describe the message in one to three sentences.

3. Do you agree with the message expressed in the cartoon? Why or why not?

4. Does the cartoon support the author's point of view in any of the readings in this publication? If the answer is yes, be specific about which reading or readings and why.

5. Are any of the readings in Chapter Four in basic agreement with the cartoon?

IMMIGRATION REFORM

- See the following summaries of 1996 laws that have reformed immigration in major ways, and drastically limited public assistance for immigrants by many billions of dollars.

- Two major pieces of legislation dealing with immigration were passed in the 104th Congress. **The Welfare Reform Act**, H.R. 3734, contains provisions that curtail benefits for legal aliens and denies most benefits for illegal aliens. This bill was signed into law by President Clinton on August 22, 1996.

- "The welfare law...strips most federal assistance from undocumented immigrants once and for all. It bars most legal immigrants from food stamps and Supplemental Security Income, and gives states the option to cut them off from Medicaid." (**Star Tribune** of Minneapolis, Nov. 18, 1996.)

- On September 28, 1996, Congress passed H.R. 3610, the Omnibus Appropriations Act for Fiscal Year 1996, which incorporated the provisions of H.R. 2202, **Immigration in the National Interest Act**. The primary objective of this bill is aimed at controlling illegal aliens. President Clinton signed this bill on September 30, 1996.

A. ALIEN ELIGIBILITY FOR BENEFITS UNDER THE NEW WELFARE AND IMMIGRATION LAWS[1]

Introduction

Comprehensive new restrictions on the eligibility of legal aliens for means-tested public assistance were established by the major

[1]Excerpted from a **Congressional Research Service** report for Congress by Joyce C. Vialet and Larry M. Eig, Oct. 16, 1996.

welfare bill that was signed into law on August 22, 1996 (P.L. 104-193). This law, the Personal Responsibility and Work Opportunity Reconciliation Act, also broadened restrictions on public benefits for illegal aliens and non-immigrants (aliens temporarily here, e.g., to visit, attend school, or work).

Program Ineligibility

The new welfare law replaces alien eligibility standards for many federal programs, which varied, with standards that are more comprehensive and restrictive. The alien eligibility provisions of the new welfare law deny illegal aliens access to many more federal programs than under previous law. It also imposes unprecedented restrictions on the ability of legal immigrants to receive means-tested federal assistance. However, legal immigrants remain eligible for certain federal aid, including education assistance, child nutrition, and emergency medical assistance. The new welfare law allows the states to determine which aliens may receive state and local benefits, though illegal aliens may only obtain benefits under state laws passed after August 22, 1996, the date the welfare law was enacted.

The Congressional Budget Office (CBO) has estimated the alien eligibility changes in the welfare law will save almost $23.7 billion over six years, 56% of which will result from changing the eligibility rules for Supplemental Security Income (SSI) for the Aged, Blind, and Disabled. The $23.7 billion savings account for almost half of the $54.1 billion savings estimated for the Act.

B. SUMMARY OF "ILLEGAL IMMIGRATION CONTROL AND IMMIGRANT FINANCIAL RESPONSIBILITY ACT OF 1996"[2]

Title I - Improvement of Border Control, Facilitation of Legal Entry, and Interior Enforcement

- Authorizes the hiring of 5,000 new Border Patrol agents over five years, nearly doubling the current total.

- Authorizes $12 million for physical barriers including triple fencing extending 14 miles eastward from the Pacific Ocean along the southern border; improved roads; and the installation of improved equipment and technology.

[2]Excerpted from a **Congressional Research Service** report for Congress, October 1996.

- Authorizes the hiring of 900 Immigration and Naturalization Service investigators over three years to enforce alien smuggling and employer sanctions laws, and 300 investigators to investigate visa overstayers.

- Allows the U.S. Attorney General to authorize state and local law enforcement officers to apprehend, detain and transport illegal aliens to INS detention centers.

- Establishes pilot programs for interior repatriation of deported aliens, for improvements in collecting departure records of temporary visa holders, and for use of closed military facilities for immigration enforcement (detention).

Title II - Enhanced Enforcement and Penalties Against Smuggling and Document Fraud

- Increases the criminal penalties for document fraud and alien smuggling (including up to life imprisonment for alien smuggling in which a death occurs).

- Permits government to use wiretaps in investigating alien smuggling and document fraud, and makes those crimes indictable as racketeering offenses under the Racketeer Influenced and Corrupt Organizations (RICO) Act.

- Makes it a crime to make a false claim to U.S. citizenship for the purpose of illegally voting, obtaining any federal benefit or employment in the United States.

INDEX

BIBLIOGRAPHY

Magazine References

Anderson, Stuart and Stephen Moore. "GOP Breaches of 'Contract'?" **The Washington Times**, Nov. 6, 1995: A22.

Andreas, Peter. "U.S.-Mexico: Open Markets, Closed Border." **Foreign Policy**, June 22, 1996: 51.

Bethell, Tom. "Immigration, Sí, Welfare, No." **The American Spectator**, Nov. 1993: 18.

Bowles, Linda. "Illegals Striking Gold in California." **Conservative Chronicle**, Apr. 24, 1996.

Briggs, Vernon M. Jr. "Immigration Policy and the U.S. Economy." **Journal of Economic Issues**, June 1996: 371-389.

Buchanan, Patrick. "Searching for Deliverance." **Interview**, Mailer, Norman. Esquire, Aug. 1996: 54.

Corry, John. "How Does Mexico Treat Its Illegals?" **The American Spectator**, June 1996.

"Dark Refugee Picture Also Has Points of Light." **National Catholic Reporter**, May 31, 1996: 24.

deToledano, Ralph. "Immigration – The Need for Common Sense." **Conservative Chronicle**, May 15, 1996.

de Uriarte, Lynn. "Anti-Immigrant Politics." **The Progressive**, Sept. 1996: 18.

Duleep, Harriet Orcutt and Mark C. Regets. "Social Security and Immigrant Earnings." **Social Security Bulletin**, Summer 1996: 20-30.

Ehardt, Gregory J. "Why California's Proposition 187 Is a Decision for the U.S. Supreme Court." **Tulsa Journal of Comparative & International Law**, Spring 1996.

Feder, Don. "Mexican Government Is Two-Faced on Issue of Illegal Immigration." **Human Events**, July 7, 1995: 15.

"France. Keep Them Out." **The Economist**, U.S. Edition, April 27, 1996: 53.

Francis, Samuel. "Feds Intimidate Immigration Control Activists." **Conservative Chronicle**, 1995.

Francis, Samuel. "Immigration: Two Steps Forward, One Step Back." **Conservative Chronicle**, 1995.

Frey, William H. "Immigrant and Native Migrant Magnets." **American Demographics**, Nov. 1996: 36.

Garvin, Glen. "Bringing the Border War Home." **Reason**, Oct. 1995: 18.

Graham, Wade. "How the U.S. Protects the Traffic in Cheap Mexican Labor." **Harper's Magazine**, July 1996: 35.

Hart, Jeffrey. "Halt Legal Immigration While Reform Is Debated." **Human Events**, Oct. 13, 1995: 20.

Henderson, Rick. "Alien Notion?" **Conservative Chronicle**, 1995.

Henderson, Rick. "Fact and Friction." **Reason**, Feb. 1995: 16.

Hill, Robert Charles. "Immigration Reform Conservatives Should Support." **Human Events**, Nov. 17, 1995: 19.

"Huddled Masses." **The Economist**, Aug. 31, 1996: 35.

"Immigration and Politics." **The Economist**, Aug. 17, 1996: 22.

"Immigration Sweeps Hit Lodging Labor Force." **Hotel & Motel Management**, Sept. 2, 1996: 4.

Kirschten, Dick. "Immigration: Crossing the Line." **The National Journal**, Aug 3, 1996: 1620.

Lamm, Richard D. "Truth, Like Roses, Often Comes with Thorns." **Vital Speeches of the Day**, Oct. 1994.

Matloff, Norman. "How Immigration Harms Minorities." **Public Interest**, Summer 1996: 61-71.

Miles, Jack. "A Bold Proposal on Immigration." **The Atlantic**, June 1994: 32.

Moore, Stephen. "The Anti-Immigration Party." **The American Spectator**, June 1996.

Moore, Stephen. "Give Us Your Best, Your Brightest." **Insight**, Nov. 22, 1993: 21.

Reed, Lawrence W. "The Immigration Problem." **The Freeman**, Oct. 1994: 551.

Reuben, Richard C. "The New Anti-Terrorism Law Allows Border Guards to Summarily Exclude Aliens Without Documents." **American Bar Association Journal**, Aug. 1996.

Roberts, Steven V. and Anne Kates Smith. "Uncle Sam, Bar the Door." **U.S. News & World Report**, April 29, 1996: 28.

Rodriguez, Gregory. "The Browning of California." **The New Republic**, Sept. 2, 1996: 18.

Salas, Abel. "Life as a Hispanic Immigrant." **Hispanic**, June 1996: 26.

Salisbury, Carolyn S. "Are Abused and Abandoned Children the First Casualties in America's War on Immigration?" **University of Miami**, April 1996.

Samuelson, Robert J. "Immigration and Poverty." **Newsweek**, July 15, 1996: 43.

Scaperlanda, Michael. "Aliens and the Constitutional Community." **Iowa Law Review**, March 1996.

Schuck, Peter H. "Alien Rumination." **Yale Law Journal**, May 1996: 1963-2012.

Schwarz, Benjamin. "The Diversity Myth: America's Leading Export." **The Atlantic Monthly**, May 1995: 57.

Simon, Julian L. "Europe's Costly Immigration Myths." **The Wall Street Journal**, Apr. 18, 1991: 8.

Simon, Julian L. "Foreign Workers, American Dream." **The New York Times**, June 1, 1995.

Simon, Julian L. "The Nativists Are Wrong." **The Wall Street Journal**, Aug. 4, 1993: A8.

Simon, Julian L. "Why Control the Borders?" **National Review**, Feb. 1, 1993: 27.

Skousen, Mark. "Freedom for Everyone...Except the Immigrant." **The Freeman**, Dec. 1995: 592.

Sowell, Thomas. "The Tragedy of American Immigration Policy." **Conservative Chronicle**, 1995.

Weissenstein, Eric and Jonathan Gardner. "Congress Revives Immigration Plan." **Modern Healthcare**, Sept. 30, 1996: 8.

Book References

Barry, Brian and Robert E. Goodin, eds. **Free Movement: Ethical Issues in the Transnational Migration of People & Money**, 1992, Pa St U Pr.

Baubock, Rainer. **Transnational Citizenship: Membership & Rights in International Migration**, 1994, (Pub. by E Elgar UK), Ashgate Pub Co.

Campbell, Dennis. **International Immigration & Nationality Law**, 1993, Pub. by M Nijhoff NE, Kluwer Ac.

Cohen, Robin, ed. **The Cambridge Survey of World Migration**, 1995, Cambridge U Pr. Danforth, Loring M. The Macedonian Conflict: Ethnic Nationalism in a Transnational World, 1995, Princeton U Pr.

Garling, Scipio, ed. **Ten Steps to Ending Illegal Immigration**, 1995, F A I R.

George, Susan. **The Debt Boomerang: How Third World Debt Harms Us All**, 1992, Westview.

Grant, Madison. **The Conquest of a Continent: Of the Expansion of Races in America**, 1977, Ayer.

Guild, Elspeth. **The Developing Immigration & Asylum Policies of the European Union: Adopted Conventions, Resolutions, Recommendations, Decisions & Conclusions**, 1996, Kluwer Law Tax Pubs.

Hatton, Tim and Jeffrey Williamson, eds. **Migration & the International Labour Market**, 1994, Routledge.

Immigrants in the United States, 1995, HUP.

Immigration Act of 1990 (Public Law 101-649), 1994, DIANE Pub.

Jacobson, Matthew F. **Special Sorrows: The Diasporic Imagination of Irish, Polish & Jewish Immigrants in the United States**, 1995, HUP.

Jones, Richard C. **Ambivalent Journey: U.S. Migration & Economic Mobility in North-Central Mexico**, 1995, U of Ariz Pr.

Jordan, Barbara and Susan Martin. **Legal Immigration: Setting Priorities**, 1996, DIANE Pub.

Kurelek, William and Margaret S. Engelhart. **They Sought a New World: The Story of European Immigration to North America**, 1985, (U of Toronto Pr), Tundra Bks.

Lamm, R. D. and G. Imhoff. **The Immigration Time Bomb: The Fragmenting & Destruction of America by Immigration**, 1986, Gordon Pr.

Lefcowitz, Eric. **The United States Immigration History Timeline**, 1990, Terra Firma Bks.

Lockhart, James. **Spanish Peru, 1532-1560: A Social History**, 1994, U of Wis Pr.

Lukacs, John. **Immigration & Migration: A Historical Perspective**, 1986, Amer Immigration.

McDaniel, Antonio. **Swing Low, Sweet Chariot: The Mortality Cost of Colonizing Liberia in the Nineteenth Century**, 1995, U Ch Pr.

Merriman, Nick. **The Peopling of London: Fifteen Thousand Years of Settlement from Overseas**, 1994, U of Wash Pr.

Migration to the Arab World: Experience of Returning Migrants, 1990, UN.

Penninx, R., et al. **The Impact of International Migration on Receiving Countries: The Case of the Netherlands**, 1993, Swets.

Powers, Mary G. and John J. Macisco, Jr., eds. **The Immigration Experience in the United States: Policy Implications**, abr. ed., 1994, CMS.

Razin, Assaf and Efraim Sadka. **Population Economics**, 1995, MIT Pr.

Smith, Joseph W., et al., eds. **Immigration & the Social Contract: The Implosion of Western Societies**, 1996, (Pub. by Avebury Pub UK), Ashgate Pub Co.

Sowell, Thomas. **Migrations & Cultures: A World View**, 1996, Basic.

Takaki, Ronald. **From Exiles to Immigrants: The Refugees from Southeast Asia**, 1995, Chelsea Hse.

Trends in International Migration - Annual Report 1994, 1995, OECD.

Vandererf, Bob and Liesbeth Heering, eds. **Causes of International Migration: Proceedings of a Workshop**, 1996, DIANE Pub.

Walch, Timothy, ed. **Immigrant America: European Ethnicity in the United States**, 1994, Garland.

Williams, Rod. **U.S. Immigration & Naturalization Made Easy**, 1996, NW Pub.